# CREATING THEIR OWN SPACE

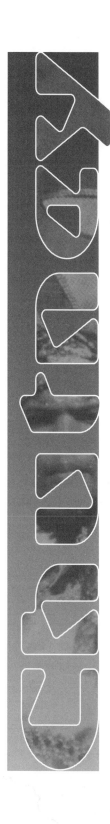

# CREATING
# THEIR
# OWN
# SPACE

## The Development of an Indian-Caribbean Musical Tradition

TINA K. RAMNARINE

UNIVERSITY OF THE WEST INDIES PRESS
Barbados • Jamaica • Trinidad and Tobago

University of the West Indies Press
1A Aqueduct Flats    Mona
Kingston 7    Jamaica

05   04   03   02   01        5   4   3   2   1

CATALOGUING IN PUBLICATION DATA

Ramnarine, Tina K.
Creating their own space : the development of an Indian-Caribbean musical
tradition / Tina K. Ramnarine

p. cm.
Includes bibliographical references and index.
ISBN: 976-640-099-7

1. Chutney (Music). 2. Music – Trinidad and Tobago – Indian influences. 3.
Popular music – Trinidad and Tobago. I. Title.

ML3486.T7 R37 2001              784.68

Set in Adobe Garamond 11.5/14
Cover and book design by Alan Ross

Printed in the United States of America

To Dad

. . . thousands of memories across the *kala pani*

# Contents

Illustrations   *viii*
Acknowledgements   *x*

Introduction   *1*

1 Tracing the Development of Chutney   *21*

2 Making the Music   *43*

3 Chutney as an Expression of Indian-Caribbean Identity   *75*

4 From Wedding Ritual to Popular Culture   *100*

5 Musical Spaces, Cultural Spaces, Social Spaces   *119*

Notes   *146*
Glossary   *151*
References   *154*
Index   *163*

# Illustrations

## Figures

Figure 1  Sketch map of India  *7*
Figure 2  Sketch map of Trinidad  *8*

## Photographs

Photo 1  Preparing for a performance: heating tassa drums to raise the pitch  *13*
Photo 2  A chutney ensemble performing at a wedding in Trinidad  *13*
Photo 3  Publicity poster for the chutney singer Terry Gajraj  *26*
Photo 4  Sundar Popo in conversation  *38*
Photo 5  The promoter Praimsingh, in his shop  *73*
Photo 6  Publicity poster for a chutney show in London  *94*
Photo 7  Publicity poster for a chutney show in London commemorating Indian Arrival Day  *95*
Photo 8  Chutney audience in London at a performance by Rikki Jai  *97*
Photo 9  Tassa drummers at a wedding ceremony in Trinidad  *104*
Photo 10 Rikki Jai singing at a chutney show in London  *138*

## Scores

Score 2.1 "Loota La", Sonny Mann  *44*
Score 2.2 "Eh Bhaiya Bhowji", Amina Ramsaran  *45*

Score 2.3 "Phoulourie", Sundar Popo  *49*

Score 2.4 "Indian Arrival", Sundar Popo  *49*

Score 2.5 "We Voting UNC", Jairam Dindial  *49*

Score 2.6 "Guyana Baboo", Terry Gajraj  *50*

Score 2.7 "Guyana Kay Dulahin", Anand Yankaran  *62*

Score 2.8 Rhythms played on the dhantal  *67*

Score 4.1 Examples of maticore rhythms  *111*

# Acknowledgements

I am indebted to family and friends in Trinidad for their generosity, hospitality and assistance during field trips. Although I do not name them here for there are so many, they all know who they are and I thank them for their continued support and interest. I am grateful also to the musicians and those involved with music who spent time exchanging ideas and discussing music with me, and to Suresh Rambaran of G and H Promotions for introducing me to chutney by inviting me to chutney events in London.

Discussions with Dr Brinsley Samaroo and Dr John Cowley have been illuminating. I am grateful to Savitri Rambissoon Sperl and to Girijesh Prasad for helping to translate some of the chutney song texts into English. Staff at the West Indies Special Collections, University of West Indies Library, allowed me access to material held there and were also helpful in pointing me in the direction of relevant sources.

This book is partly based on my published articles: "Indian Music in the Diaspora: Case Studies of Chutney in Trinidad and in London", *British Journal of Ethnomusicology* 5 (1996): 133–53; "Brotherhood of the Boat: Musical Dialogues in a Caribbean Context", *British Journal of Ethnomusicology* 7 (1998): 1–22; "Historical Representations, Performance Spaces and Kinship Themes in Indian-Caribbean Popular Song Texts", *Asian Music* 30, no. 1 (1999): 1–33.

# Introduction

The popular Caribbean music known as chutney has been shaped by historical processes that brought together a variety of musical elements. It has developed in the pluricultural contexts of the Caribbean. Through their performances and recorded repertoires, chutney musicians in Trinidad have explored the interstices of diasporized conditions: the spaces of island home and the ties of its inhabitants to the wider global ecumene. Influential chutney song texts refer to the imagery of the boat: the different ships that sailed across the other middle passage (from India to the New World). These songs offer reminders of the historical and economic circumstances that have shaped musical practice on the island and point to the difficulties of drawing musical boundaries that correspond with island identity.

Chutney has found a new performance space in carnival, together with calypso, soca and steel band. These have found audiences and performance spaces outside the island in various centres of the Caribbean diaspora and in world music scenes. Interisland movements of people and music, diasporic and touristic intercultural networks, recording opportunities and transnational music markets have played their parts in establishing performance arenas for several of the island's musical traditions that extend beyond its geographic setting. Performances in the Trinidadian context, however, are deeply implicated with political processes that relate to the island space. This book will explore how chutney serves as a vehicle for affirming a sense of multilocal belonging which is built on local and global networks of musical exchange. The book will also examine the role of chutney in articulating political aspirations to national unity and in reconceptualizing what constitutes contemporary Trinidadian society.


## SHIFTING SPACES

The musical scene on board the clipper ship *Sheila* provides a starting point for exploring the development of chutney. The *Sheila* was built in Glasgow and sailed from there for Calcutta in March 1877 with a crew of thirty-two and a load of manufactured goods for trade with India. From India the ship was to travel to the Caribbean with a new load: the "bound coolies" or indentured labourers heading for the sugar plantations of Trinidad. The captain of the *Sheila* on that voyage was W. H. Angel. His diary of the voyage, published as a retrospective account in 1921, provides one of the few eyewitness testimonies of this post-slavery triangular trade that had been developing since 1838.

In his text there are references to the musical activities of the sailors (singing sea shanties) and of the Indian migrants. His observations of Indian music begin on arriving in Calcutta and his descriptions focus on the strange and different qualities of the Indian musical expressions that he heard. In the following he comments on the music performed at an Indian dignitary's wedding: "the native taste for music is peculiar to European ears. The more din and discord, bang and clash, as much of the big drum, or tom-tom, as strenuous arms and hands can get out of those instruments of torture, the more the applause" (Angel in Ramchand and Samaroo 1995, 53).

Angel had occasion to recall the music he had heard at the wedding once he had set off for the Caribbean with the indentured labourers on board. He writes that:

to prevent quarrelling or plotting mischief . . . the coolies were encouraged to keep themselves amused in their own fashion. This mostly resolved itself into tum, tum, tumming on their small drums – the same sort of affair that I have described in the doings at the Baboo's (the Indian dignitary's) wedding. The tunes they get out of those tom-toms, to European ears, is most dreary, tuneless, and monotonous; but the natives at times work themselves up to a high pitch of excitement . . . It is said, and with truth, you can always fathom the thoughts of the native mind by listening to the performers on their tom-toms. (Angel in Ramchand and Samaroo 1995, 65)

In Angel's comments we detect those familiar polarized, binary oppositions between the colonizer and the colonized, us and the other, the familiar and the exotic, the European and the native, the civilized and the savage. He cites Kipling: "East is East, and West is West, and never the twain shall meet", a citation which is all the more telling since it follows his evidence of musical interaction during that voyage. Having arrived in Trinidad, Angel writes about the disembarking of the coolies:

On leaving, my crew awoke the echoes by giving them no end of cheers, and several rousing shanties. The coolies, at the start of the voyage could not make out what that kind of singing meant, it being so strange to their ears; but towards the end, it was amusing to hear their attempts to join in. They never accomplished it – the melodies were not Eastern enough for them; even in that it is as Kipling puts it, "East is East, and West is West, and never the twain shall meet." (Angel in Ramchand and Samaroo 1995, 106)

Yet the Indian labourers on board the *Sheila* were clearly engaging in processes of musical interaction in learning the crew's sea shanties. Angel's simple model of cultural flows focuses on a relation of domination in a one-way process of musical interaction – on the colonizeds' absorption of the colonizers' expressions – but this is questioned by his own earlier passing remark that: "At Calcutta several of my boys and crew had possessed themselves of various kinds of musical instruments" (Angel in Ramchand and Samaroo 1995, 70).

In Angel's account, musical difference is posited despite evidence of musical exchanges. A century after the voyage of the *Sheila* which Angel writes about, the popular music of Indians in a postcolonial Trinidad offered a clear challenge to notions of "eastern" musical properties and was beginning to have a significant impact in public and political forums. By the 1990s, the popular music known as "chutney" had emerged as a central medium through which the negotiation of political concerns, questions of identity and the experiences of diaspora and postcolonial sensibilities could be articulated.

Music plays an important role in the Caribbean. As in other cross-cultural performance contexts, music and dance in the Caribbean often "provide the means by which the hierarchies of place are negotiated and transformed" and music is "socially meaningful because it provides means by which people recognize identities and places, and the boundaries which separate them" (Stokes 1994, 4–5). The role that chutney assumes in relation to expressions of religion, identity, ethnicity, gender, politics and social commentary finds many diverse counterparts throughout the Caribbean region. Jamaican reggae, for example, is linked with Rastafarianism and Cuban bembe is a santeria (Yoruba-derived religion) event. Zouk (from Martinique, Guadeloupe, St Lucia and Dominica) is seen as a symbol of identity and nationalism and a means for creating a sense of unity between Creole speakers from these islands (Guilbault 1993, 109). Calypso song texts generate heated political debates which are frequently carried out through the print media.

In Trinidad, I heard music almost wherever I travelled: in maxi-taxis, in private cars, in markets, in the rum shops, at the beach – and somewhere, somebody was listening to the radio. The importance of music is such that debates about local music are debates about local culture. It provides one of the main forums for learning about contested ideas of culture. Debates about chutney are tied together with those that explore diaspora experience and the "quest for national identity" (Van Koningsbruggen 1997).

Just as the clipper ship *Sheila* highlights the shifting spaces in which musical interactions and creative innovations take place in relation to a discourse of musical difference, so too are musics of the Caribbean characterized by their "hybrid" qualities, and people forge identifiable genres by incorporating musical ideas from many sources. In this sense, Caribbean musics can be seen as precursors to the phenomenon known as World Music. Yet, as with so many musical traditions, these hybrid Caribbean musics are always tied to places and mark specific identities. *Son* and rumba are Cuban, parang is Spanish Trinidadian, ska and mento are Jamaican, and merengue emerged as a national symbol of the Dominican Republic during the early twentieth century. Chutney is identified as an Indian-Caribbean genre, yet it too displays influences from diverse sources. Whereas some musical elements can be traced to India and can be analysed as examples of musical retention or preservation, others have emerged as a result of cultural interaction in the pluricultural contexts of the Caribbean. Chutney musicians draw upon ideas from Indian folk traditions, devotional songs and film music, as well as from calypso, soca and rap. Because the boundaries that mark places and identities through performance of chutney are compromised by these musical interactions, they are continually being negotiated in creative and performance endeavours and in public discourses.

The kinds of creative musical interactions that were evident during the voyage of the *Sheila* and that are a characteristic of chutney are central to Stuart Hall's vision of a diaspora experience that can be defined "by the recognition of a necessary heterogeneity and diversity; by a conception of 'identity' which lives with and through, not despite, difference; by hybridity" (Hall 1996, 120). Such a conception of identity is reiterated by Stuempfle in his study of the Trinidad steel band. He too writes about musical hybridity and notes that the willingness of pan musicians to draw on the variety of musics available to them has led to the fabrication of "a new and distinctively local music" and that in fact, the "dynamics of cultural creativity have been the basis of the creolization model of Caribbean society" (Stuempfle 1995, 220). Creolization as an indigenization process leads to the perception of patterns identified as African or as Indian "less as ethnic properties than as actions that anyone may employ in appropriate situations" (Stewart in Stuempfle 1995, 220).

Several studies have shown that cultural and social life in the Caribbean has been profoundly affected by the Indian presence and by the traditions that Indians maintained in a new geographic context. Considerable attention has been paid to the historical, social and economic experiences of Indians in the Caribbean (for example, Klass 1961; Wood 1968; Dabydeen and Samaroo 1987, 1996; Vertovec 1992). While musical practices have also come under scrutiny, the focus has been on the preservation of Indian musical traditions in a diasporic context and the extent to which repertoires have been retained (Myers 1998). Such preoccupations were shaped in part by anthropological concern with cultural cohesion as well as by Indian-Trinidadians' own efforts to maintain their links with India. These links were maintained either through kinship contacts or through a continuing interaction with the former "motherland" and with the maintenance of their ancestors' cultural practices. Yet the processes of reproducing culture in diasporic contexts, just as in the ancestral land, have resulted in cultural transformations of various kinds (see Vertovec 1992 who focuses on kinship, caste and Hinduism), rather than the preservation of "Indian culture" from nineteenth century India.

In this book I provide an ethnographic and analytic account of chutney, looking at the role of music in shaping an Indian-Caribbean identity in local and global arenas and at what current popular sounds

can tell us about contemporary Trinidadian society. The major characteristics of this genre will be pointed out in exploring what makes it both
distinct from and yet comparable with other Caribbean musics.

The ethnographic data was mainly collected during fieldwork trips to
Trinidad from 1990 to 1996, so the analysis is therefore specific to the
Trinidadian experience. But I will also briefly look at chutney in London,
which is where I first came across this genre, to emphasize my argument
that chutney contributes to the experience of diaspora as multilocal. I will
discuss how chutney on public stages contributes both to performances
of belonging in Trinidad and to a diasporic imagination that looks to a
former homeland but which is based on generalized images of
"Indianness". The example of London is important in this respect
because in this context we find people participating in chutney shows in
affirming a diasporic identity that looks to a homeland in the Caribbean.
First I turn to historical perspectives in introducing questions about how
chutney developed and how it is linked to issues of identity and ethnicity
in Trinidad.

## INDENTURESHIP AND THE EMERGENCE OF AN INDIAN-CARIBBEAN IDENTITY

In tracing the development of chutney and the emergence of an Indian-
Caribbean identity, we can begin by considering population movement
from India to the Caribbean following British imperial policies to replace
the workforce on sugar cane estates in particular.

Both in Britain and in the colonies themselves, the question of labour
dominated discussions on the future of the West Indian sugar plantations, following the emancipation of slaves in 1838. The colonial
Caribbean cane-sugar industry, with the labour of African slaves, had
expanded to such an extent during the eighteenth and nineteenth
centuries that what had once been a rare commodity had become a daily
consumer product (see Mintz 1985). But after 1838, the emancipated
slaves deserted plantation agriculture on the terms and conditions
prescribed by the planters and by the British government, unwilling to
work "for their former masters for wages instead of lashes" (Williams
1964 [1962], 86). To maintain the colonial plantation system of sugar
production, labourers were recruited from other parts of the empire.
Between 1838 and 1917, more than half a million Indians were taken to

the Caribbean as indentured (contracted) labourers, changing the whole population pattern in the West Indies (see Figures 1 and 2). British recruiters in India told prospective labourers that "they would be going to Chini-dad (land of sugar) or that Fiji was a place just beyond Calcutta" (Samaroo 1987, 28). Indian labourers, neither realizing the journey which lay ahead of them nor understanding the contracts which they signed, saw indentureship as a way of escaping harsh economic conditions and hunger, and anticipated an easier life in new lands. Some of them did not sign contracts. They were simply kidnapped. The system of indentureship, strikingly similar to the system of slavery that preceded it, was criticized in turn and gave rise to anti-indenture campaigns (Samaroo 1987).

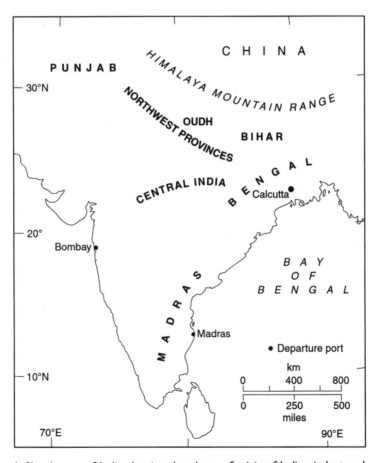

*Figure 1: Sketch map of India showing the places of origin of Indian indentured labourers who travelled to the Caribbean*

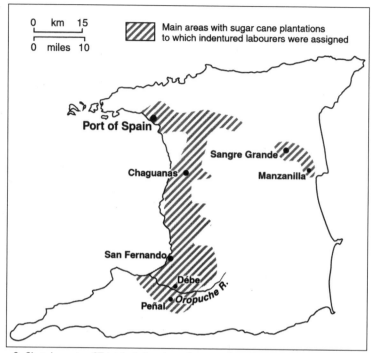

*Figure 2: Sketch map of Trinidad showing places referred to in the text*

The first ship transporting Indians to Trinidad was the *Fath Al Razak* which landed in Port of Spain in 1845 (Samaroo 1995).[1] On board were two hundred and twenty-seven Indians. Their contracts initially lasted for a period of five years after which they could work for a further five years in order to claim a free return passage to India. When indentureship was abolished in 1917, less than a quarter of the Indian labourers returned to their homeland. Most of them decided to exchange the passage to India for a grant of land, for as Cudjoe observes, "so much had the quality and reality of their experience changed that there was really no home to which they could return" (Cudjoe 1985, 19). "Chinidad" had become Trinidad.

Today, Indians as an ethnic group form nearly half of the island's population. Yet it is not a homogenous group, for the Indians came from different regions, spoke different languages and dialects, were members of different castes, and brought a variety of cultural practices with them. Examples of the retention of cultural elements from India to Trinidad have been located in kinship systems, village structure and religious rituals (Klass 1961), and in clothing, food and language (Lowenthal 1972). The majority of indentured labourers came from the northern provinces of Uttar Pradesh and Bihar where Bhojpuri was spoken. The Bhojpur tradition, therefore, which had produced religious heroes such as Rama, Krishna and Buddha, as well as the epics, the *Ramayana* and the *Maha Bharat*, became dominant in Trinidad.

The preservation of religious ideals and the celebration of religious festivals were significant in maintaining a sense of ethnic and cultural identity. Music has continued to play an integral role in religious rituals. Traces of ritual music can be found in some chutney songs. As well as the preservation of traditions, new ideas imported from India (including religious movements and figures) are absorbed by Indian-Caribbean populations. The notion of musical revitalization is pertinent therefore to the analysis of chutney too. Films (subtitled in English) have been imported from India since the 1930s and have made an important contribution to the chutney style. As well as imported film music, Indian musicians and religious leaders who teach Indian classical music (in particular) have travelled to Trinidad. Some of the most influential figures included the Hindu missionaries from the Bombay-based Arya Samaj reformist movement who visited Trinidad during the 1920s;[2] Professor Adesh who has visited repeatedly since the 1960s and has now set up a religious movement in addition to teaching North Indian classical music; and the Sai Baba religious movement which was introduced in 1974 (see Myers 1993a, 238–39). Devotional music, hitherto unknown in Trinidad, has been introduced through such movements. Indian communities in Trinidad have looked to such influential figures for ideas as to what is truly Indian. The comments of these figures about Indian-Caribbean culture in relation to the "parent" one have stimulated debates about authenticity. Also, since the 1940s, several dancers from India, or dancers who have been trained in India, including Rajkumar Krishna Persad, Satnarine and Mondira Balkaransingh, Pratap and Priya Pawar, have held workshops and classes in Trinidad teaching the classical Odissi style and Punjabi, Gujurati, Bihari and southern Indian folk dances. Tracing the development of chutney is complicated by such exchanges, for some Indian elements, then, are not examples of retention at all, but are new ideas which are incorporated in constructing a Caribbean "Indianness". The means whereby performance traditions have continued to be transmitted from India to a Caribbean diasporic context have been diverse and include mass media systems, movement of people through cultural and religious programmes, and provision of formal learning situations.

The demise of certain traditional practices was equally significant in the formation of an Indian-Caribbean identity. Language and the feudal caste system broke down. In Trinidad, labourers from different castes, from Brahmins (high caste) to Chamar (low caste), lived next to each other in the barracks and worked together in the cane-fields. English, which had been established as the official language of British India by 1835, emerged as the common language which enabled Indians in the English-speaking Caribbean to communicate with each other and with the rest of the populace. The experience of indentureship in Trinidad led to the development of a sense of ethnic solidarity which has been some-what ironically characterized by Sam Selvon as "East Indian Trinidadian West Indian" (Selvon 1987, 21). Here is a statement of ethnic identity that demonstrates allegiances to India as the ancestral country of origin, to the Caribbean island Trinidad which is "home", and to the Caribbean region in general. By drawing on elements from different traditions, chutney reinforces these loyalties and affirms the identity of Indian-Caribbeans as Caribbean people of Indian origin. Even where commentators assert that the tradition is Indian, the assertion is made in a context in which being "Indian" serves both to remind Indian-Caribbeans of their ancestry and to further local political debates and interests.

## THE STUDY OF MUSIC IN THE DIASPORA

Although chutney draws upon traditions that came to the Caribbean with the first indentured labourers from India, the first public performances of this genre took place in Trinidad as recently as the late 1980s. Some efforts had been made to introduce the music into the public arena during the 1970s (for example, through the performances of the chutney singer, Sundar Popo), but these did not attract large audiences. Chutney shows are also presented, and are gaining increasing popularity, in London, New York and Toronto – metropolitan centres in which Indian-Caribbeans have settled. There are some musicians in India (for example, Babla and Kanchan) who perform chutney, having incorporated Caribbean popular forms in their repertoires. Their largest audiences, with regard to chutney, are nonetheless in the Caribbean – in Trinidad, Guyana, and Suriname – places with significant Indian-Caribbean populations.

While tradition is often perceived as stemming from and having close ties to particular localities, the relationship between tradition and place is questioned when a single tradition is maintained, developed and changed by people in several different geographic contexts. With which place can a tradition like chutney be associated? India, the Caribbean or the urban centres around the world that have become "home" to Indian-Caribbean communities? Human mobility and migrants as carriers of traditions to different places have expanded the ethnomusicological frame of reference, which commonly studies music in its cultural context in a specific geographic location. The shift in emphasis has led to questions about the survival of elements of tradition in new contexts, and the ability of music to retain its identity away from the culture from which it sprang (Reyes-Schramm 1990). Although recent ethnographic accounts have examined music and musicians in the context of migration from rural to urban centres (for example, Stokes 1992; Turino 1993), much research remains to be carried out on the topic of music-making in the diaspora. Projects tracing the roots of African music in the New World (Herskovits and Herskovits 1947; Levine 1977; Small 1987; Alleyne 1988; McDaniel 1998) provide models for similar undertakings in the field of Indian music in the diaspora. Yet the complexity of music-making in diasporic contexts lies in the immense variation between different examples. For example, over 150 organizations were interviewed for the anthology, *Klangbilder der Welt*, produced by the International Centre for Comparative Musicology, a study which revealed an enormous "range of approaches and histories of formation, activity, and stylistic choice" among what Slobin calls the "diasporic intercultural networks" found in Berlin (Slobin 1993, 66). The complexity and density of these diasporic intercultural networks and the circulation of popular musics through them preclude any simple perceptions of a diasporic experience.

The focus in this book will be on how ideas about music history relate to an Indian-Caribbean diaspora experience by offering people ways of remembering and reconstructing the past. "Some aspects of the past are stories waiting to be told," writes the American musicologist, Treitler (1989, 163). The stories which make up histories are not only depictions of the past, however, but also documents of the present (Treitler 1989, 174). Waiting to be told, these stories are, too, the narratives that will shape future understandings of history. Different representations of the history of the musical tradition, chutney, can be seen as reflecting "contested ideas of local culture" (Olwig and Hastrup 1997, 10). In analysing chutney, notions of history, space and place emerge as significant markers for such contested ideas in which the locale is the

Caribbean. Thus chutney is represented as having its origins in the *mathkor* ceremony, a ritual space which was the preserve of women, and a cultural practice that emerged from India. But chutney as a popular genre is identified with Indian-Caribbean communities and is used on local and global stages as an expression of Indian-Caribbean identity. What were once female musical spaces have become female and male spaces. While *mathkor* is "Indian", chutney is specifically "Indian-Caribbean". Some local commentators speak, however, in terms of the contribution that chutney makes to Indian as well as to Caribbean music. Chutney is frequently evaluated in terms of the reception accorded to it in India. Place and space are important in asserting and maintaining links to India and an Indian cultural heritage. I shall explore the question of chutney's status as Indian music in the diaspora. This involves delving into the history of the tradition and into how chutney's history is represented by Caribbean commentators.

## Towards Contextualizing Chutney

Chutney has emerged recently as a distinct genre and it invites a mixed reception. Some people regard its performance with disapproval and even with horror. Others enjoy dancing to the music. For many listeners, chutney overshadows other types of Indian-Caribbean musics. Yet, in many performance contexts, chutney is heard alongside other Indian-Caribbean forms. In searching for the origins of chutney, I attended wedding ceremonies to hear traditional folk songs. Often the songs that I went to hear only played a small role in the musical event. The wedding ceremonies themselves, however, provided opportunities to hear Indian-Caribbean musical microcosms.

Preparations for a wedding in a small village in south Trinidad were extensive. Men put up a wedding tent at the front of the house. Women cooked food (kneading dough for *roti* [bread] and making sweets) in a large open-air kitchen at the back of the house. Many different kinds of musics were heard at the wedding. Women sang traditional wedding songs in Bhojpuri. The *pundit* (priest) chanted ritual songs. A *tassa* (drum) group announced the arrival of the main participants in the wedding ceremony. The drummers heated their *tassas* to ensure that the pitch would be high enough as the last preparations for the wedding were taking place (see photo 1). A few men gathered around the *tassa* group to dance. An orchestra (keyboards, *tassa*, *dholak*, *dhantal*, harmonium, singer) had been hired for the occasion, too (see photo 2). The orchestral

Photo 1: *Preparing for a performance: heating* tassa *drums to raise the pitch*

musicians performed Indian popular and film songs. A sound system blasted out the latest chutney sounds and a young girl performed a solo chutney dance. A group of local schoolgirls also performed dances from an Indian film to music played from recordings.

The wedding provided an overview of the kinds of Indian-Caribbean and Indian musics to which people in the village listen. The following Saturday was market day in the village. Chutney was played over stereo systems but dub, club mixes, reggae, rap and chart hits also featured in

Photo 2: *A chutney ensemble performing at a wedding in Trinidad: left to right,* dholak, harmonuim *and* dhantal

the musical soundscape for shoppers bargaining and exchanging pleasantries with traders.

While chutney was played as part of the musical entertainment at the wedding ceremony in which "Indian" traditions were emphasized, it is a popular genre that is often heard alongside other contemporary Caribbean musics. Indeed, I argue that it is a genre that has emerged from the interaction between "Indian" and diverse Caribbean musics. Such interactions are not only a vital part of a particular experience of diaspora but also lead to a consideration of how music is categorized or labelled in specific ways in the construction of difference. How music is labelled is often linked to distinctions posited between musics and the histories claimed for them.

Captain Angel wrote about musical differences between "East" and "West" to emphasize a separation between colonizer and colonized. Chutney's status as a contemporary popular cultural form challenges notions of separate "Indian-" and "African-" Caribbean musical cultures often found in the literature on Caribbean musics.[3] An emphasis on chutney's "Indianness" exists, however, in contexts in which such a musical and cultural background continues to be neglected. While many recent texts portray, or at least acknowledge, a complex scenario of social and musical interaction between ethnic groups in Trinidad (Constance 1991; Reddock 1995; Cowley 1996), there are studies which overlook an Indian contribution to Caribbean culture. Hill (1993), for example, adopts the metaphor of "calaloo", a soup made up of contrasting ingredients, in his study of the diverse influences which have shaped calypso. It is a particularly appropriate metaphor for a Caribbean music. He nevertheless dismisses any Indian contribution to the form from the outset. "Cultural contributions to calypso came from other groups," he writes. If an Indian contribution to calypso cannot be totally dismissed, he continues with the proviso that "when people with an East Indian cultural background contributed to calypso, they did so as Creoles, not as East Indians" (1993, xiv). Similarly, Hebdige's study of culture, identity and Caribbean music focuses almost exclusively on "African-Caribbean" genres (reggae, in particular). His mention of other ethnicities in the Caribbean, such as Chinese and Syrian, is brief. Moreover, marking out an "Anglo-Indian" ethinicity in the Caribbean is flawed (since Indian migrants to this region were not generally drawn from "Anglo-Indian" communities). The distinctions drawn in these studies between ethnic groups and their contributions to Caribbean music are in sharp contrast to other views in which interaction is highlighted. Wood, referring to Simmonds's (1959) book on the steel pan, for example, suggested that it was probably through the drumming, the ritual function of the chamar caste that "the drum-beats of India were drawn into the mainstream of Trinidad music. Their techniques are part of the inheritance of the steel bands" (Wood 1968, 144). In a study of the steelband, Stuempfle (1995, 219) similarly identifies several musical influences, including a tassa contribution:

The steelband is essentially a culmination of a long process of musical creolization, a process in which diverse musical traditions have been locally re-created. Among the many sources of steelband music are Afro-Trinidadian tamboo bamboo, metallic percussion, and Orisha drumming; the calypso tradition of vocals and string-band accompaniments, which itself is a creole synthesis of African, French, Spanish, and British musical elements; Indo-Trinidadian *tassa* drumming; European marching band and classical traditions; Afro/Latin dance rhythms and tunes; and North American popular songs and jazz.

While many musicians claim to be producing chutney music, "chutney" actually means different things to different people. Choosing terminology for the purpose of analysis is thus a complicated process. I use the umbrella term "chutney" to refer to all music that is described as such. There are, however, various types of chutney that should be noted here. A few eminent performers insisted that the term properly refers to music that is played by a group comprising voice, *dholak*, *dhantal* and harmonium. The addition of any other instrumental timbres, particularly brass and electronic instruments, signifies branches of chutney, commonly, chutney soca (or soca chutney) or more recent experiments like ragga chutney. The term chutney soca is an attempt to indicate the relation between chutney and soca. Similarly, ragga chutney indicates links between ragga and chutney. The insistence on specific instrumental timbres for the performance of "chutney" proper represents a somewhat purist attitude to the genre. As will be seen, performers who describe these distinctions between categories of chutney are themselves involved in changing the tradition of chutney. They take chutney into new performance contexts, and cross the boundaries that determine who performs the music and the function of performance.

When I first started researching chutney there was very little ethnographic or analytic material available. One of my interests was in tracing the development of Indian-Caribbean popular music. My preoccupations stemmed from the view that a contemporary genre like chutney can only be understood in a historical context. While Myers (1984) and Desroches (1996) have undertaken important research into Indian-Caribbean music, there is no general history of Indian-Caribbean music, even though this music offers an interesting case study into the workings of musical traditions in diasporic contexts. If Indian-Caribbean music has received scant attention in ethnomusicological literature, this is in contrast to writings on music in India itself, which has a long history, with a particular abundance of theoretical treatises. British colonial writings on Indian music in India are also plentiful and include descriptions of art and folk traditions (see Myers 1993b; Jhairazbhoy 1993). There is also a growing literature on Caribbean music. Recent studies include Manuel's (1995) general text on Caribbean music, Guilbault's (1993) ethnography of zouk, Hill's (1993) study of calypso and calypsonians and Cowley's (1996) historical account of the development of carnival, canboulay and calypso.

The main bibliographic sources available to me included press reports, Constance's (1991) book in which chutney is mentioned in relation to calypso and Ribeiro's (1992) examination of chutney. One of the earliest references to the genre is found in Ahyoung's dissertation where mention is made of women's songs known as *chatni* (1977, 73), more commonly known today as chutney. (I have chosen here to follow contemporary convention.) In Myers (1984), a study based on her fieldwork in Trinidad over the period 1974 to 1977, references to the genre are rather fleeting. A passage in which she relates a conversation in which she specifically asks about chutney provides, however, a good example of the dialogic nature of the research process:

Sankey was stretched out in the hammock by her house, her morning's work completed.

"Come naa, come naa Helen," she said. Sankey was acknowledged to be the finest lady singer in the village [Felicity], and a good drummer as well."

"Come lime naa. Come eat crabs naa."

"Sita Raam," I said. The curried crabs were brought out and I lay back in a second hammock.

"I need a coke bottle to smash these," I said. (The villagers cracked them with their teeth.)

"Mash it, mash the crab for she," Sankey called out, and the crabs were taken away.

WHAM WHAM from the kitchen, and then my lunch was returned. The curry sauce for the crabs was very hot, and my eyes watered.

"Sankey," I asked, "how do you make pepper sauce?"

"Well, we make pepper sauce with pepper and acid," she replied, "cooking acid."

"Sankey," I asked, "when they talk about hot songs, when they talk about chutney songs . . . "

"Chutney sauce?" she asked.

"No, songs."

"Oh, songs, songs! Yes, yes. I know what you mean. A hot song is when you beating the drum hard. And the ladies singing, you know, that they sing on a good voice then, big voice. Well, that is chutney song." (Myers 1984, 101)

More recently, Myers (1993a) and Manuel (1995) mention that chutney is an emerging popular genre, but more detailed descriptions and analyses of this tradition are only now being undertaken. The literature noted here thus represents only a beginning to research in this field. Such have been the developments in the World Music market, however, that during the process of revising my own manuscript, chutney has very quickly been introduced into the arena of scholarly discourse about Caribbean musics. Written accounts dealing specifically with chutney have appeared alongside its current popularity. In a revised and updated account of field research in Trinidad, Myers (1998) includes a chapter on chutney, focusing on song texts, in her study of songs from the Indian diaspora. Her informant, Amar, who was largely interested in maintaining traditional practice, did not view chutney favourably. "It's not a form to be proud of but it is sweeping across Trinidad these days," he told her (Myers 1998, 368).

If there is still, nevertheless, a paucity of written material, early sound recordings of Indian-Caribbean music are also scarce. Spottswood and Cowley's "Discography of East Indian recordings from the English-speaking West Indies" (1996) indicates that there were no recordings made under this category of musical performance during the period 1915–1939 by the main recording companies, Bluebird, Decca and Victor.[4] During my field research I found no commercially available recordings made before the late 1950s (although my search for such recordings was not extensive). Examples of Indian-Trinidadian musical performances are found amongst Alan Lomax's 1962 recordings. These include music heard at a Hindu wedding in the village, Debe in south Trinidad (Rounder 11661–1723–2).[5]

There are three main reasons for the paucity of material relating to chutney, one of which is indeed the general lack of documentation on Indian music in the Caribbean. The second is that chutney as public performance is a recent phenomenon. Although it is well known in the Caribbean and in the United States and Canada (especially in New York and in Toronto), and to a certain extent in Latin America, it has not yet established its presence in the market of world music. In Britain, for example, commercial recordings of chutney (produced in the Caribbean and in the United States) were not readily available until the mid 1990s and were usually bought from private vendors. This remains the case towards the end of the decade. Third, many practitioners regard chutney as drawing upon traditions which were performed by women for audiences of women at gatherings such as *mathkor* and *lawa* (pre-wedding celebrations in which Mother Earth is honoured and rice is parched to be used in the wedding ceremony) and also at *chatti* and *barahi* (ceremonies which take place six and twelve days after the birth of a child). Knowledge of *mathkor* (which I shall focus on in this book) was, and still is, passed on following the patterns of oral transmission. Women's traditions are often difficult for ethnographers to access (Koskoff 1989). Yet this is not a secret tradition. The lack of empirical data and historical research is also a reflection on the general inattention paid to the experiences of Indian-Caribbean women (Poynting 1987).

## OUTLINE OF THE BOOK

The themes of identity, traditions in the diaspora, gender, and the ways in which musical histories are constructed are intertwined in this book. Chapter 1 outlines some of the historiographical and methodological problems encountered in examining Indian-Caribbean musical traditions. I provide examples of the dialogic nature of the research process by including transcripts of interviews with three chutney singers. The comments of the singers that appear in those interviews are found later on, interspersed with my own narrative. In including this interview material I have been guided by the kinds of ethical issues relating to giving voice to ethnomusicological informants and my concern has been to include some examples of the testimonies of chutney practitioners alongside my own subsequent reflections.

Chapter 2 is concerned with the musical aspects of chutney: with melodies, rhythms, texts, structure, instrumentation and musical transmission. How is the music put together? What are the Indian musical models it draws on? How does an instrument like the *dhantal* provide a means whereby people can reflect on historic experiences? This discussion of chutney's stylistic features leads to questions about how music and memory are bound together in articulating particular identities and in forging distinctive performance arenas within a national space.

In chapter 3, chutney is analysed in relation to issues of ethnicity, identity and musical practice in the national forum. Music is often closely tied to people's sense of identity and also identifies groups of people. Chutney is an example of the ways in which music operates as a marker of identity since it has been associated primarily with Indian-Caribbean populations. In exploring discourses of musical identification, I discuss chutney song texts as commentaries that deal with kinship themes and diasporic experience and that therefore help to create a sense of relatedness.

Although the origins of chutney are unclear, it is a genre that draws upon folk and ritual traditions from India. In particular, chutney is represented as having its origins in the Hindu wedding ritual known as *mathkor*. Chapter 4 examines this historical representation which connects *mathkor* with chutney. Since *mathkor* was mainly a female mode of expression, the relation between *mathkor* and chutney provides both a focus for a consideration of women's performance and a framework for examining issues of gender. Beyond the framework of women's performance, the dominant historical representation of chutney's origins in *mathkor* tells us about social interactions at a local level and about assertions of a Caribbean "Indianness".

In the final chapter, the question of chutney's status as Indian music in the diaspora is revisited. Since diaspora and history are themes that are central to the forging of postcolonial subjectivities, I turn to postcolonial theoretical frameworks to focus on contemporary intersections between ideology and music history. These intersections contain an evaluative dimension, for as Goodman (1998) notes in relation to political articulation throughout Africa, postcolonial projects have often involved an assessment of the effects of colonialism. Historical representations are vital too in this respect, for a second dimension resulting from critical assessment of colonial heritages is the "rediscovery of the value of [one's] own cultural heritage" (Goodman 1998, 205). While chutney has emerged in part from Indian folk traditions, its importance lies in the role that it plays in modern, postcolonial Caribbean contexts. As a musical tradition, then, chutney is both Indian and Caribbean, and in fact it emerges as a cultural expression which delineates a specifically Indian-Caribbean space.

# Tracing the Development of Chutney

I posed the question, "Where did the name chutney come from?" The singer, Rawatie Ali, told me, "You make chutney with coconut or mango and mix it with peppers. It's a hot tasting thing and because the music is hot too people started calling it chutney" (personal interview, 12 July 1996).[1] James Ramsawak, singer and teacher, said, "There is no music called chutney. Chutney is a food. In my conception the word chutney came into use from Moean Mohammed [who was involved with setting up the competition, Mastana Bahar, which is a display of competence in Indian performance traditions]. The word in Hindi is *lahara* and that means something spicy . . . Chutney is a fast beat song normally sung by women in days gone by and in those days it used to be called *lahara*. So the music would be called *lahara*" (personal interview, 30 July 1996).[2] According to yet another commentator, the dancer, Satnarine Balkaransingh, when women started dancing at celebrations like weddings, "They would start dancing normally and then somebody would say, 'Give us some *chatak*.' *Chatak* means spice, so spice it up, make it *chatak*" (personal interview, 13 July 1996).[3]

A comparison of some of the answers I collected in response to the question of the origin of the name, chutney, demonstrates the variation in people's notions of the history of this musical genre. These diverse accounts highlight some of the historiographical and methodological issues that arise in tracing the development of chutney.

## ORAL TESTIMONIES, HISTORIES AND CULTURAL CHANGE

Given that one cannot turn to a large body of literature or to sound recordings from the more distant past (before about 1939), finding people who not only remember but are also able to relate their musical memories provides the researcher with source materials. These oral testimonies are invaluable in attempting to record and reconstruct past Indian-Caribbean musical practices. In fact, finding and speaking to people who are willing to share their experiences and knowledge of music is a standard methodological approach adopted by ethnomusicologists. In studying past as well as present traditions the task is further complicated beyond the location of people willing to share knowledge. Many of the people I wished to interview were elderly. They were the ones who held memories of the past. Yet they were also, in some cases, not always in good health, so access to them was restricted, although not denied. Such conditions render the fieldworker increasingly sensitive to the question of intrusion. Those who study orally transmitted traditions with a focus on the past commonly face this methodological issue. A striking example from the Trinidadian context is Moodie-Kublalsingh's (1994) oral record of the Spanish-speaking Trinidadian community, the so-called cocoa panyols. In her study, Moodie-Kublalsingh presents accounts that she collected from Spanish-speaking peasants born around the turn of the century, and reveals a sense of documenting a rural culture in its twilight years. Such fieldwork conditions give rise to the ethnomusicologists' lament that the musical traditions of older generations which are left unrecorded will be lost to succeeding ones – a concern with some justification for musical change can be rapid. The example of the cocoa panyols in Trinidad finds resonances amongst Indian-Trinidadian communities. While chutney has been foregrounded in public national discourses, a host of other musical traditions, which are held in the memories of older generations, seem to be receding.

The fact that musical traditions do change and are not static adds, too, to the historiographer's concerns. In the past four years in Trinidad, for example, the situation regarding the transmission of Indian music on the radio has been transformed. While Malm and Wallis reported in 1992 that East Indian music had not been "integrated into the regular flow of music on the radio" (1992, 69), there were three radio stations by 1996 which regularly transmitted Indian and Indian-Caribbean music.

As well as giving rise to concern about the disappearance of some traditions, such rapid change also offers the possibility of developing theoretical perspectives on notions of continuity and change. Moodie-Kublalsingh concludes her study with the following observations:

On the one hand, as I travelled around with my tape recorder, it seemed that I was certifying the demise of Trinidad Spanish. Yet, at the same time, I was witnessing at close range the dynamics of cultural change and the durability and pervasiveness of the Trinidad Spanish parang within our small heterogenous nation. But very little of that cherished Hispanic culture could ever be retrieved on a simple tape recorder. Much more would persist in the lives and minds of the children of the disappearing 'cocoa panyols', provided that the younger generations were sufficiently receptive and positive in their attitude to the old culture. (1994, 222)

Similarly, the ways in which people relate to chutney show how they are both forging links with "older" traditional forms as well as leaving a performance space open for creative innovations. The rise of chutney seems to provide an example of rapid cultural change but it is also a marker of the "pervasiveness" of Indian heritages in Trinidad.

A general issue arising from the use of oral testimonies to write a music history is the extent to which a few individuals can give insights into a musical culture. Just as I collected different accounts of the origin of the name, chutney, I collected different histories of chutney from different people. These differences stemmed from varied perspectives and perceptions of the past, varying individual experiences and memories, and, sometimes, an inability to remember, which left some accounts incomplete. How, then, does one as historiographer and ethnographer select material to include in a musical history of chutney from the multiple and sometimes conflicting accounts collected?

Contemporary Indian-Caribbean musicians who are trying to learn the musical traditions of older generations face the same difficulties as the researcher. As one singer told me in relating how she learnt songs that used to be performed at Hindu wedding ceremonies:

I went to old people in the village [Debe] who knew the songs. It took me about a year to compile these songs because, you know, the old people sometimes they tell you "I remember a verse and I forget the next verse" . . . Anytime I got some time I used to go by them [the older singers] and I used to keep on writing. They used to sing and I wrote. Sometimes when they're singing they'll give you the first verse last and the last verse first. You have to think about it after you've writ-ten it down and put it in order. (Rawatie Ali, personal interview, 12 July 1996)

Rawatie Ali went to the old singers in Debe who could give her ideas about the performance of Indian-Caribbean songs in the past. Yet she does not just reproduce what she hears. For the analyst, the lack of sound recordings from the more distant past raises a major methodological problem in conceptualising musical continuity and change. Without experiencing the sound qualities of the traditions through time, it is difficult to compare corresponding traditions and the processes of change that they have undergone in different geographic contexts. The emphasis is necessarily placed, then, on seeking signs of "preservation" or points of similarity." These difficulties mean that depictions of musical histories and notions of musical continuity and change assume increased signifi-cance in analysing how histories which are partly "imagined" inform contemporary social and cultural interactions.

The historiographical and methodological problems encountered in tracing the development of chutney can be summed up as follows:

1. few written accounts or early sound recordings;
2. difficulties in locating people who hold and can relate requisite knowledge (memories) of earlier Indian-Caribbean musical prac-tices;
3. inconsistencies in oral testimonies;
4. lack of documented evidence to support claims put forward in oral testimonies;
5. musical change.

Some common themes do emerge, nevertheless, providing a framework for a historical account of chutney. In Trinidad, the history of Indian-Caribbean music, encompassing the genre now known as chutney, begins with the arrival of the first indentured labourers in 1845. They brought Indian music, particularly folk and religious songs with them. From the variety of musical traditions which came to the Caribbean from India, both the songs and dances performed by women at wedding celebrations and at the birth of a child are often identified as being the precursor to chutney (Ramaya 1990, 2; Rawatie Ali, personal interview, 12 July 1996; Satnarine Balkaransingh, personal interview, 13 July 1996; Cecil Fonrose, personal interview, 22 July 1996). Some commentators specifically locate the origins of chutney music and dance style in the *mathkor* ceremony – the religious ritual and celebration which takes place on the Friday night of a Sanatanist Hindu wedding.[4] These traditions were primarily a female mode of musical and dance expression and were performed in private contexts. "Chutney" was not the term used in referring to these performances. The name "chutney" came into general use with public and stage performances of this music and dance form. One of the first recognized chutney performers was Sundar Popo who, himself, claims to have been at the forefront of the genre's emergence: "I am the first one who created chutney singing" (Sundar Popo, personal interview, 22 July 1996).

Despite the variations in oral testimonies, each view deserves consideration and springs from valid foundations. Common threads in different accounts can be identified, such as the linking of chutney with folk traditions. These threads provide the basis for reconstructing Indian-Caribbean musical history within interpretative frameworks. Moreover, the project of collecting these testimonies will itself provide material for future accounts of Indian-Caribbean music.

The remainder of this chapter presents examples of the dialogic process in field research. I include these examples to highlight two important points regarding, first, analysis and the establishment of ethnographic authority and, second, different approaches to representation. Collecting accounts of chutney in Trinidad, which themselves reveal diverse perspectives on the genre, has played a central role in shaping my own reflections. Rather than list all those who have contributed to the formation of my analysis, I present extracts from recorded conversations with three chutney singers, one of whom is a Guyanese performer who regularly gives concerts in London, and two who are Trinidadian. In ethnographic accounts, these types of data are usually interspersed with the main text, which is of course the ethnographer's voice. In according this material a central place at the outset, my aim is to further the current ethnomusicological aim of letting people speak about their own music, as Myers puts it: "finding ways of helping native observers . . . describe their own music" (1993b, 13). Guilbault sets an example by including chapters written by local commentators in her study of zouk. These chapters then provide material for the author's analysis (Guilbault 1993). Since my interview material has been collected, following ethnomusicological methods in the field, from conversations, both formal and informal, the transcripts below illustrate the research process as well as document "native" descriptions.

## Dialogues

In the first dialogue, the chutney singer Terry Gajraj makes a number of important observations regarding the links between biography and creative processes. He discusses the stylistic features of the genre and highlights the significance of timbral qualities, of instrumentation, in defining and marking "chutney" elements. While he relates this popular music to a ritual context, like so many other commentators, he does not draw a straight genealogy from *mathkor* to chutney. However, he does talk about how he explores this relation in one of his own songs. A final main topic in this dialogue is the kind of political awareness he exhibits and his location of chutney within a wider Caribbean complex. He draws a parallel between chutney and reggae and refers to the notion of "consciousness".

Photo 3: Publicity poster for the chutney singer Terry Gajraj (reproduced with permission)

*1. Tina K. Ramnarine in conversation with the Guyanese singer Terry Gajraj (London, 29 May 1996).*[5]

**TKR:** When you are making up a chutney song, where do you get your ideas from?

**TG:** Well, personally, when I do a song, the ideas, like for the lyrics, I think back to Guyana. I think back to Guyana. Let's say "Guyana Baboo" for instance. Not too many people have written songs about Guyana: the love for their country, at least in a chutney style. People have done like in other styles – reggae and stuff like that. So I just wanted to try something *that* way and in all my songs, or at least most of them, I try to bring one or two expressions from back home, or some words or something, you know. I visualize like back home [sings], "me come from de country they call Guyana, land of de bauxite, de rice and sugar". Those are the basic things that people identify with. Guyana is a land of sugar plantations and rice fields and all of us know somebody there, maybe our parents, or *chacha*, uncle, or whatever. They are cane cutters or work on rice farms like my grandfather did, and, you know, that's one instance. And "Tun Tun Dance" now that's different in terms of, I think back to the movies we used to see – and I thought she was very funny and I always try to use a little humour in my songs or in most of them. So I thought of Tun Tun, she's so funny everybody enjoys her movies and all of that. So then I wrote that song about her and all the songs are like that. I think of topical things. I think about back home you know.

**TKR:** So they are things which have a special significance for you then, and they remind you of Guyana and things you are familiar with?

**TG:** Yes. And you know, after you've left the country it's like you always have this longing to go back and longing for things there, and I noticed when I brought my songs out, I think one of the main reasons the response was so good was because nobody ever sang something like that, about Guyana, and it made people feel (and this is what I heard from people) it made them feel like, you know, they think back to home and you get that feeling, that warm home feeling.

**TKR:** So you make up the lyrics yourself and also the music?

27

**TG:**    Yes.

**TKR:**    Do you write it down or do you do it by ear?

**TG:**    Like, you see, I drive a lot and I have one of these [points to my cassette recorder], a smaller one, a dictaphone. Most of my writing I do while I'm driving between New York and Connecticut.

**TKR:**    And so you just put it straight onto tape . . .

**TG:**    . . . and I put it onto the tape and like when I'm flying like [to] England, to here, I did a song.

**TKR:**    Did you?

**TG:**    Yeh, always. And if I try, if I think and say, okay, I want to write a song, I never do. It just comes. Like maybe I'm listening to another song or I'm reading something and there's an idea right there, and I say, oh I'll use that, I'll build a song around that. It just happens like that.

**TKR:**    So it doesn't take very long?

**TG:**    For me, personally, no. But once I have that idea and I have like four, five verses, I always find that the longer I take to record it the more I add to it and the more verses I write, and finally I go into the studio with twelve verses and the guys kind of help me out as to "let's take that one – it's catchy" you know, or something like that.

**TKR:**    Do you think your musical style has changed in the last few years?

**TG:**    Maybe in little bits but I think the general direction of the music, like as in chutney, has been the same.

**TKR:**    So is chutney the real sort of focus of what you do, because I know you've done soca as well haven't you?

**TG:**    Yes, soca and reggae.

**TKR:**    And religious songs?

**TG:**    Yes, and I'll be bringing out a religious album pretty soon too.

**TKR:**    But chutney is the thing that you really like?

**TG:**    Chutney is my main thing, yes. I find it a lot easier for me. I've done reggae songs just so – to appear for the younger crowd . . . because a lot of parents, I mean especially in Canada, they came up to me and said, "Our children never listened to chutney music before" – and by the way, I should mention something to you – back home in Guyana, I don't know if you know, we used to call it "local" music: l-o-c-a-l. Up to this day people still call it local music.

**TKR:** So they don't think of it as being Indian music, they think that it is local music?

**TG:** Yes, in Guyana. But of course because it was the same thing that the Trinidadians were doing, and the Trinidadians were calling it chutney . . .

**TKR:** Do you know how that name got used?

**TG:** Chutney?

**TKR:** Yes, who started using the name chutney?

**TG:** I really don't know but I mean it's something that I can easily research and I mean when you go to Trinidad you could talk to the same people who I would actually talk to. But I suspect that Drupatee, that singer, she has a lot to do with it if I can remember well, because I think she was among the first to actually use that name . . . Okay, this is "chutney", soca chutney or something to that effect. But it's easy to go back to check, I mean she has it on her records and stuff like that.

**TKR:** So because this music comes from, you know, these folk traditions and things that women were using in their, like in the pre-wedding celebrations, did you still call it local music or did you just call it by the name that the ceremonies have?

**TG:** No. They call it local music. No-one like called it "maticore" [*mathkor*] until I just wrote that down, just so, once again, to get that word out there – maticore – but people used to just keep it in circles, you don't see it written in any newspapers or anything, it's just that they call it maticore.

**TKR:** So it's not that it used to be called – the music itself was maticore and now it's called chutney . . .

**TG:** No. Definitely not. They wouldn't even call it maticore, you know, because the maticore was something like totally different. I mean they would regard it as that Friday night thing [taps rhythm]:

you know, that beat there, you know it's such a simple beat, and people used to laugh at it – oh, you know she doesn't know [how] to play the drums, you know, that's why they play like that. It was like an infectious rhythm and I just decided to try something with it.

**TKR:** So your chutney songs are related though, because you use that kind of rhythm?

**TG:** Yes, but not in all of them . . .

**TKR:** . . . but not in all chutney songs . . .

**TG:** . . . no, not in all of them.

**TKR:** So chutney is actually something different. It's not necessarily part of the ceremony at all.

**TG:** No.

**TKR:** So what is it related to? Is it like calypso or . . . ?

**TG:** It does have a calypso tempo you know, and I would say – I don't really know, I really can't put a finger to it, but I know it has a calypso tempo. They go about the same tempo like 1/30, 1/35. Chutney tends to go faster, but I noticed in the past year that the calypso also . . .

**TKR:** . . . is speeding up?

**TG:** Yeh. Most of the calypsos are like between 1/30, 1/35, 1/40, 1/45. Chutney you know they have gone to 1/55 and that's like the norm. You know, like the real chutney singers, in Trinidad they call it "classical". Alright, I mean we don't call it "classical" back home, we usually call it like "tan" singing . . .

**TKR:** . . . so there are lots of different strands. It's not so simple then. Chutney is not a whole phenomenon which you can say, oh that music is chutney . . .

**TG:** . . . I think that maticore is just another part. The maticore beat, it's just another part of chutney, but it's more Indian you know. It has a more Indian feel because you don't have the calypsos or the soca sound. You have that [taps rhythm]:

But not all the songs go with that beat either. A lot of them go with the regular soca beat [taps rhythm]:

And then the *tassa* does [taps rhythm]:

like how the cowbell would go, on the soca beat [taps rhythm]:

If you imagine the beat it would be like 2/4.

**TKR:** But then is chutney like . . . is it just a popular genre? A recent one? Because the name wasn't used before, I think 1980 or something, the 1980s. Or had you heard the name before?

**TG:** Yeh, I think you're right where that is concerned, as to the name "chutney". But that style of music . . .

**TKR:** . . . has been going on for ages?

**TG:** Oh yes. Since I was born.

**TKR:** So you've been familiar with it?

**TG:** Yeh I've been familiar with that beat, but like in Guyana, for instance, they just recorded it as a kind of novelty thing, and what recording did they do? Just recorded on a regular tape-recorder, like you have here. This would probably give you a better quality than what they used in those days . . . And another thing they would call the songs, right, was "rum-shop" songs.

**TKR:** So they weren't just the wedding tent songs, they were rum-shop songs.

**TG:** Yes, you know, the men would go to the rum-shop, order bottle and glass, and hit the table and sing [taps table and sings]:

*nana de lecha kai . . .* [?]

I mean a guy in Trinidad, he approached me, he was like, I want you to do something and he had this idea, let's call it "Rum-shop Medley". Because all, well not all, most of the songs were just what people used to sing just for kicks you know. You feel nice and you just sing something and then, I mean, like Sundar Popo heard it and he goes 'ah, that sounds good', take it, write a song around it, you know, add in some more lyrics, like phoulourie chutney and stuff like that.

**TKR:** Is there a lot of interaction between chutney in Guyana and in Trinidad?

**TG:** Interaction in terms of?

**TKR:** You know, like do you get influences between, do people in Trinidad and in Guyana, are they influenced by each other, what they're doing with chutney?

**TG:** Yes. I think now there is more of that. Like the Guyanese are being influenced by the Trinidadians because it's more commercial. But before that they never really looked at it that way.

**TKR:** So they were just doing their own . . .

**TG:** . . . They were just doing their own thing and I think that innocence, that music, and the simplicity of it, you know, Sundar took a lot of that, Sundar Popo, and quite a few other Trinidadian singers they go over because as you know Guyana had no recording studios, nobody records anything, I would never have had a chance if I hadn't left Guyana and gone to New York. You know, maybe someone would have come and taken my songs as well. Because, I mean they do nothing with it and because they have just like basic portable stuff. They have like an A track, something called "Hala Gala [?] Studios". That's the name of it, "Hala Gala". It's a black guy, black Muslim guy married to an Indian lady, and I forget what his name was, Faroukh something, Omar Faroukh I think is his name, and he is the one that recorded a lot of old, the real old, original Guyanese songs then, from Hala Gala Studios.

**TKR:** So recordings before 1950 even?

**TG:** Possibly. I don't want to tell you the wrong thing. Possibly. But I know I grew up and I heard certain songs. The recordings were very lousy I heard, most of them, like I said, if you were recording on this [points to my tape recorder] you'd get much better quality.

**TKR:** In your last recording when you were doing these calypso songs and you said to me that you had been trying to add some chutney elements into it – what were these, what do you think were those chutney elements that you were adding to the calypso?

**TG:** Just the *dholak* [drum] and the *dhantal* [an iron rod struck with a horseshoe shaped beater].

**TKR:** So it's just the instrumentation?

**TG:** The instrumentation, yes. It was basically the instrumentation, everything else was, just that, but I just tried a thing because right now like chutney awareness is kind of up. I figured it would be interesting, you know, here's a soca song with chutney beat and something that people, they probably know, yes it could go, it all depends how you play it. You don't play the drum the traditional way as you would normally play it, but you're thinking okay, high hat. You know the high hat goes [taps on the table] same thing with the *dhantal*. You know you release. The closed high hat is like when you go with the *dhantal* – open high hat and you release it [demonstrates]. Basically very simple.

**33**

**TKR:** What do you think about Mighty Sparrow's incorporation of Indian themes like in the song "Marajhin" where he adds the *dhantal* as well? Do you think it's the same sort of thing that you are doing?

**TG:** Yes, yeh, basically it's the same thing and like when Lord Shorty did way back. It's just a matter of experimenting with it, you know. They did, you know, there was like a protest and stuff like that because they did lyrics, you know, "Marajhin" and things like that. But all those were really interesting concepts. That is the thing for you to make your music interesting. You have to keep doing different things. And they experimented going back to the old. I think everything goes in a cycle. After a while what's old becomes new and becomes old again.

**TKR:** In New York, when you play there, do your audiences think that you're playing or singing Caribbean music, or do they think it's Indian-Caribbean?

**TG:** Definitely not Indian. Definitely not Caribbean.

**TKR:** So it has to be Indian-Caribbean.

**TG:** Indo-Caribbean, yes. I can tell you about two things: the clubs and the radio. When I first went to the clubs (Indian-owned and everything), the only way they had people going to those clubs was to play soca or calypso. At the end, say three or four o'clock in the morning, they would put on one or two Indian songs and the Indians would go and do a little thing and have real fun. Gradually, as chutney started, it has gone full circle. Now it's all chutney music and a few calypsos and soca in those same clubs. With the radio stations now, they used to play Indian songs from India . . . but now there are radio stations that are dedicated to just playing chutney. In the past, if you wanted to play chutney people would scoff at you. Our own people were embarrassed by it. People would just play it at home. But now, even radio stations that just play Indian music have had to introduce some chutney to have a listenership.

**TKR:** So why is chutney so popular now?

**TG:** I think it's related to the general scene. If I draw a parallel with reggae, reggae used to be just conscious lyrics, like Bob Marley, they call it "culture", "consciousness", whatever. Then came the dancehall. I think the Indian music was equivalent to that culture, that consciousness. Indian music was that soothing thing you know and chutney came like a real rock-up thing and that's what the young people wanted. Young people used to just listen to reggae or dub and those kinds of dance music, but now they have something "Indian" which is sung in Hindi and English and they can understand it and relate to it.

---

*2. Tina K. Ramnarine in conversation with the (African-Trinidadian) singer Cecil Fonrose (Trinidad, 22 July 1996).*[6]

In the second dialogue presented here, Cecil Fonrose takes up some of the themes discussed in the preceding example. He talks about his involvment with calypso as well as with chutney, about the origins of chutney and about changes in instrumentation in contemporary chutney practice. He also provides an example from his own repertoire of a chutney song composed by him that deals with current political themes.

**Tina K. Ramnarine**: What is chutney and where did it come from?

**Cecil Fonrose**: As far as I know, chutney started with Indian singing – ladies songs – things like *barahi* night [celebrations on the twelfth night after the birth of a baby]. So the ladies get together and they have their fun singing these songs. Now after that, men take it up and start because the beat is a faster beat than the regular classical songs.

**TKR**: What kind of beat is it?

**CF**: Chutney is like soca beat music, it's a fast tempo. Classical song was slower, you could hardly move and dance around with a classical song.

**TKR**: Why did the men start taking over the music?

**CF**: Well, ladies sing men's songs too?

**PG** [an observer]: True true.

**CF**: They just take the faster beat. The same classical songs that men used to sing before, they now put it in a faster beat and say chutney.

**TKR:** Do you know who first started using the word "chutney"?

**CF:** Well chutney is a spicy thing you know. Instead of saying spicy you say chutney. I think the first person I heard using this word was Moean Mohammed.

**TKR:** How did you become involved with chutney?

**CF:** I really start singing classical songs through a friend of mine who was a [*dholak*] drummer. The first chutney song I sang was "Ram Bolo" [1979], but then it was just a local song, only last year we call it chutney.

**TKR:** How do you compose a chutney song?

**CF:** Sometimes something comes into your mind and you want to sing a song about it. Sometimes I sing in English and I mix English and Hindi. Sometimes when I want a new song it mostly come[s] in Hindi. I don't know where and how it does come but I accept it. I never used to take copies.

**TKR:** You kept it by memory?

**CF:** Yes. This is one song I wrote and used in the Chutney Soca Monarch Competition [shows me a song text].

**TKR:** This year?

**CF:** Yes.

**TKR:** [Looking at the text] You were talking about Basdeo Panday in this song, can you read it out?

**CF:** [Reading] . . .
(Come my friends let's go, let's go and plant cane, let's go and plant cassava.)
Some playing *tassa*
some playing pan
I driving my gaari [car]
like Dan in a van [a line from a nursery rhyme].
Everyone was watching and very few did know,
Basdeo Panday came Prime Minister
and that was a really big show.

**TKR:** So when you're making up lyrics you think about things from your own experience, things from your environment here, the current politics, and what you were learning as a child – all those things?

**CF:**   Exactly so.

**TKR:**   How did you turn to Indian music, was it because you are from this village [Barrackpore]?

**CF:**   I don't know. I was involved with calypso earlier on. Then some youths came and said, "Let us try to arrange an Indian band." And I said, "No problem, I'll try it." And I tried it and I never looked back after that.

**TKR:**   What kind of instruments do you have accompanying your songs?

**CF:**   Long time [ago] I had harmonium, *dholak*, mandolin, *dhantal*, shac shacs and all that. But nowadays with this modern type of singing it's mostly electrical instruments: synthesizer, electric guitar, trumpet and saxophone.

**TKR:**   Do you still use a *dholak* and *dhantal*?

**CF:**   Yes, that doesn't be out of it, but very rarely these days we have a harmonium.

---

*3. Tina K. Ramnarine in conversation with the chutney singer Sundar Popo (Trinidad, 22 July 1996).*[7]

In the third example, Sundar Popo provides evidence of the ways in which individual biographies give credence to particular constructions of music history. He joins in the discourse of musical difference to assert his own contributions. He locates former musical practice in classical styles and he emphasizes his role in highlighting folk repertoires. Another significant point that he makes deals with questions of appropriation and creative process. Appropriation is also important in his account in the circulation of musical material from Trinidad to India. He thus points to the ways in which Indian-Trinidadians depart from the simple model of being only "preservers" of culture.

**Tina K. Ramnarine**:   Who made up this word, "chutney"?

*Photo 4: Sundar Popo (left) in conversation. Chutney publicity material from his own collection is displayed behind him.*

**Sundar Popo**:  Chutney is fast tempo music and long time ago most of the singers used to sing only classical songs. Classical singing didn't have the chutney style. In those days, the old generation understood a little Hindi and the broken language our forefathers brought from India. So they only had a classical style until I came out with some of the folk songs from India – a series of fast tempo songs. Since then everybody has started composing chutney style music.

**TKR**:  Did you actually use the word "chutney" to describe your songs?

**SP**:  Chutney is something peppy, hot. We put our common language to it because – if you make mango and put a hot sauce on it, it go have a good flavour and it comes from that, you know, something tempo, something hot.

**TKR**:  How do you compose a chutney song?

**SP**:  First of all you must have a tune and a story. A song must be based on a story. Most of the chutney singers today don't have a story, they just doing whatever they want to with beat and melody.

**TKR:** Do you make up the melodies yourself or do you borrow melodies from other places?

**SP:** It is opposite. Everyone who is singing chutney today, they follow my melody. Lots of chutney singers now are taking my melodies because I was the first one who went and do chutney. They don't have a chutney song without my melody, they take a piece, a piece, a piece, even in Indian films they use my melodies.

**TKR:** What instruments do you include?

**SP:** If you singing in a show and you have a big band you might be singing a chutney melody but it is soca music. Chutney comprises *dholak* drum, *dhantal* and harmonium. When you got that flavour you are doing chutney.

**TKR:** So if you just have *dholak*, *dhantal* and harmonium that's chutney?

**SP:** That's chutney.

**TKR:** If you add any other instrument it's soca?

**SP:** It's soca. Anytime you sing chutney with a big band it's "chutney-soca".

**TKR:** What kind of musical training did you have?

**SP:** My father is a musician. He is a *tassa* [drum] man. When I was very small, most of the time on Friday or Saturday night, they [both his parents] were going to weddings to play *tassa*. My mother had a group of ladies who used to sing at the farewell night [part of the wedding ceremony]. As young children, they couldn't leave us home so they took us with them . . . when you small and you go – Indian music and melody – we've grown with that. The love of music came then. I started playing with a band in Barrackpore when I was eight years old. When I was fifteen, I started singing [Indian] film songs, and then local songs. The first one was "Nanee Nana".

**TKR:** Did you have any influences from James Ramsawak?

**SP:** James Ramsawak was my guru. He is my guru. We won many competitions together. He is the guru of many artists in Trinidad who have made themselves famous. I was the first one, then Drupatee, Heeralal Rampartap (with [the song] "Chutney Possy"), Lilly Ramcharan and many more. The artists that he really put out, I think most of them made a name for themselves.

**TKR:** In your song, "Phoulourie Bina Chutney", you have these nursery rhymes, "Jack and Jill went up the hill" and "Little Jack Horner sat in a corner", and then something about the cane fields. What's the meaning of that song?

**SP:** Well, it's just a chutney song. It don't carry great meaning. It's [a] rhyme: "Me and my darling was flying in a plane, the plane catch a fire and we fall inside the cane." It brings many meanings and it's how you will interpret it.

## Interpretations, Fictions, Ethnographic Authority

These singers contributed, with their discussions and insights, to many of the themes which are explored in the following chapters: the history of chutney, the ways in which people identify with this tradition, men's and women's musical activities and musical change. Sundar Popo told me that the meaning of a song is determined by my interpretation of it. His statement contains the critique that analyses of such collected testimonies are also subject to interpretation, a point that has been stressed in much recent reflexive anthropological writing (for example, Clifford 1988). If Guilbault's (1993) text on zouk highlights individual interpretation, another text on a Caribbean music makes the point abundantly clear that such interpretations are also fictions of a sort. These fictions raise questions of ethnographic authority. In his book, *Salsa: Havana Heat, Bronx Beat*, Hernando Calvo Ospina (1995) writes his own accounts about this popular music from different imaginary perspectives. His study includes chapters written from the fictitious perspectives of African-Cuban, Puerto Rican (in New York) and Colombian narrators. Yet his account is lent authority by being endorsed by salsa practitioners (Celia Cruz and Willie Colon). Their appreciative comments are prominently placed at the beginning of the book. In another example from the literature on musical practice in Trinidad (Myers 1998), the tensions between writing ethnography as fiction and ethnographic authority are highlighted because of the accompanying ideology of viewing informants as ethnomusicological partners rather than as subjects of study. Myers writes that eventually what Westerners think of non-Western music may be overshadowed by what the people we have studied think of their own music. Finding ways of helping native observers, literate or illiterate, to describe their own music – their likes and dislikes, their sense of the beautiful and the ugly – is a present task for ethnomusicologists, perhaps an ethical responsibility. (Myers 1993b, 13)

In her own ethnography, however, a narrative technique that clearly establishes the ethnographer's authority over the multivocal ethnographic evidence is adopted. Her informants sometimes display a remarkable lack of historical and political awareness. For example, Myers writes:

In August, Trinidadians and Indians (and many other members of the Commonwealth) celebrate their Independence Day.

"Independence. That is the 31st August," Tara explained. "That is the day Trinidad get Independence. I don't know from where."

"From England," I said.

"Oh," she said. "They just give them a public holiday. Schools get eight weeks holiday for Independence . . ." (Myers 1998, 87)

This dialogue is an ethnographic representation that is not typical of the kinds of discourses that I came across in a postcolonial and independent Trinidad and Tobago. It contrasts with the reflective statements of the chutney practitioners presented above and with the cultural, historical and political texts of many chutney songs.

Nevertheless, the emphasis on diverse perceptions and under-standings of cultural expressions and on representations of culture as fictions that characterize these works on Caribbean musics is not coincidental. It perhaps springs from Caribbean experiences, from a consideration of the "social frameworks created for culturally diverse migrant peoples who were subjected to centuries-long processes of mostly forced cultural change" (Mintz 1996, 297). Where changes in "culture" have been the outcome of unequal power relations, of imperialism, of the concerns of global markets, of social and cultural interactions that take place in contexts constantly in flux, of creative musical impulses – cultural phenomena assume more than just symbolic importance. Many Caribbean musics have become the sites of being and being known in the world. They are musical expressions in which answers to questions about the relation between past and present must be understood as part fictions. The dialogues that I have included here already show diverse perceptions of an Indian-Caribbean musical tradition. The diversity is, as we shall see in later chapters, essential to national, diasporic and postcolonial discourses. Before turning to that discussion, the next chapter will look at the stylistic features of chutney and at how the music itself is put together.

# Making the Music

The singer, Sundar Popo, emphasized the importance of a song's melodic and textual features: "you must have a tune and a story" (personal interview, July 1996).[1] While the Indian classical musician Adesh claimed that in India, different texts have different tunes (Myers 1984, 382), Sundar Popo was concerned that "his" melodies were appropriated by others:

everyone who is singing chutney today, they follow my melody. Lots of chutney singers now are taking my melodies because I was the first one who went and do [sic] chutney. They don't have a chutney song without my melody, they take a piece, a piece, a piece, even in Indian films they use my melodies. (Personal interview, July 1996)

## MELODY

Sundar Popo's view that other singers do not always compose original melodies is (indirectly) reiterated by Patasar who writes that chutney "is limited to very few tunes" (1995, 82). Whatever the origin of a particular melody, Popo's concerns point to the idea that melodies can be borrowed. Indeed, the melodic material of Sonny Mann's well-known song, which is sung entirely in Bhojpuri, "Loota La" ("Let Us Roll Together", 1995) is an example. A similar melody is heard in Amina Ramsaran's song, "Eh

Bhaiya Bhowji" (brother's sister-in-law), which was recorded by the record retailer, Praimsingh (no date given on the recording). Melodic similarities between these two examples are reinforced by the similarity of the song texts, too. The main differences between Sonny Mann's and Amina Ramsaran's treatments of the melody lie in the tempo (as presented in recorded performances) and in the rhythmic aspects which are determined by the syllabic settings (compare Scores 2.1 and 2.2). In collaborating with calypsonians General Grant and Denise Belfon Sonny Mann himself produced a chutney/calypso variant of "Loota La", which incorporates some English translations.

*Score 2.1: "Loota La", Sonny Mann (my transcription; transposed to C major for comparison with Score 2.2, original in F-sharp major). It is important to note that all transcriptions are included as guides for analytical reasons and only certain elements are considered in these examples.*

*Score 2.2: "Eh Bhaiya Bhowji", Amina Ramsaran (my transcription; transposed to C major, original in D-flat major).*

To investigate further whether contemporary ideas about melodic material correspond to folk practice in north India during the nineteenth century, Popo's and Adesh's notions about tunes can be compared to

vidence from that period. The evidence is provided by
n who presents the perspective of an "outsider". Grierson
in the British civil service – the officiating magistrate of
the 1880s. Although he was particularly interested in
ning language (he undertook the production of a Bhojpuri
grammar and a Bihari dictionary), he commented on the melodic
material of Bihari and Bhojpuri folk songs in two articles published in the
*Journal of the Royal Asiatic Society of Great Britain and Ireland* (1884 and
1886).

"You must have a tune and a story," said Sundar Popo. Grierson
indicated that the concern with melodic shape, with the tune, determined structural matters (at least in terms of metre and setting a text).
He wrote:

The peculiarity of all these songs [Bhojpuri folk songs] is that the fetters of
metre lie upon them very loosely indeed . . . the melody to which they are sung
is the only guide, and so long as the accent or musical ictus is provided for, the
author cared little whether his syllables were long or short. (1886, 209)

But if he informs us that melody was the only guide, Grierson confounds
us with his observations on melodic variety:

Every stout young fellow has a repertoire of them [short songs], out of which he
sings when he has nothing better to do, whether alone or in company. He has
probably only one tune, to which he fits all his words . . . This paucity of
melodies has often struck me. In the country districts I never heard of a new
tune being invented. There seems to be a certain stock of tunes ready made, to
which the words of every new song must be fitted. (1886, 210)

If Indian-Caribbean popular music forms have some of their origins
in these folk traditions, Grierson's nineteenth century account seems to
accord with Patasar's criticisms about the lack of melodic variety in
contemporary chutney. However, while Grierson states that he "never
heard of a new tune being invented", Sundar Popo's testimony provides
clear evidence of melodic composition. This is in stark contrast to
Marcus's claim regarding contemporary north Indian folk traditions that
there is "no melodic composition" and that neither performers nor
composers compose new melodies (1992, 101). His claim can be understood in relation to the influence that Grierson's work exerted on the

formulation of his own ideas. An acceptance of Grierson's observations allows his interpretation of "no melodic composition" being a "long-standing tradition". Marcus's perception of a new north Indian folk song is thus a new text set to a pre-existing melody (1992, 102). Yet Marcus's own case study contradicts such a bold view of no melodic composition. Marcus's case study revolves around examining the incorporation of new melodic material from film music into the folk tradition.

In writing about *biraha* in north India, Marcus notes that since the 1940s, singers have been experimenting with mixing *biraha* melodies with melodic material from other folk tunes and from Bombay film music. Reasons for borrowing the melodies of film music included the wish to appear modern and trendy. Regional, rural and caste affiliations reasserted themselves, however, and *biraha* musicians began to identify where their tunes came from in performing. Film and folk melodies were preceded by verbal explanations about their origins. These changes are related to changing social contexts, to the wish to be both modern and to be identified with Bhojpuri rural culture (Marcus 1992, 105).

The parallel with chutney is evident. Musicians and their audiences wish to be recognized as being both Indian and Caribbean. Processes of acculturation, borrowing and incorporation as a result of culture contact in a pluricultural context can be traced in the development of chutney as an Indian-Caribbean tradition. If it is a tradition that has been both preserved and changed in Trinidad, popular and folk musics in India have also undergone adaptation and change in interaction with other musical influences. This is particularly true of Indian film music itself. In its early stages, Indian cinema "borrowed extensively from Hollywood and European productions", but it has developed as "a home-grown domestic entertainment form guided by indigenous aesthetics and conditions" (Manuel 1988, 173). This is not, then, a mere imitation of Western cinema, just as chutney is not simply a reproduced Indian tradition. The emphasis in film music has been on producing simple and catchy tunes, and this in turn has influenced regional folk music. Links between chutney and Indian popular musical forms, via the film industry, can be noted here. In addition to being the dominant category of popular music in South Asia, film music also reaches audiences throughout the Indian diaspora. Diatonic melodies to which Western styles of harmonization can be added, as well as the combination of Indian instruments such as the *dholak* and the *tabla* (drum pair) with Western ones, are characteristic of popular forms both in India (Manuel 1988, chapter 7) and in the Caribbean.

In the composition processes there are parallels between contemporary Bhojpuri and Indian-Trinidadian practices, for they both turn to film music as a source of creative inspiration. In the Caribbean context, the availability of Hindi films has had a significant impact on the development of "local" culture. Manuel (1997–98) notes that Hindi film music "has for several decades been the single most popular kind of music among Indo-Trinidadians and Guyanese, despite their limited ability to understand the songs' lyrics" and that "in many Indo-Caribbean homes and workplaces, Hindi film music is playing constantly, whether from cassettes, videos, or . . . broadcasts by Indian-owned radio stations" (p. 23). These are the musical sounds that inform and influence chutney composers like Sundar Popo. Such has been the impact of these films on Indian-Caribbean creative and performance forums that in talent competitions "local film singers are typically praised not for their originality, but as the 'Voice of [film singer Mohammed] Rafi', or as 'a true imitator' " (p. 24).

The melodic range of chutney songs generally falls within an octave. Melodic movement by step and recurring melodic cells which revolve around a central note are also general features. The chorus of Sundar Popo's song – "phoulourie bina chutney"– provides an example of step-wise movement and a melodic cell which revolves around the note G (Score 2.3). Compare with Popo's song "Indian Arrival" (Score 2.4), where there is also step-wise melodic movement and a focus on the note C-sharp (which is not the tonic but the dominant). The use of such cells may lead singers to believe that their melodic material has been borrowed when, in fact, such cells are a feature of this repertoire. Consider the chorus of Jairam Dindial's political chutney song "We Voting UNC [United Nations Congress]" (1995), which contains a similar melodic cell (Score 2.5).

All of the melodies in these examples are diatonic. In fact, using the harmonium as an accompanying instrument encourages diatonicism. If the harmonium's part does not always correspond exactly to the singer's line, it nevertheless follows the vocal line closely, sometimes very slightly anticipating the vocal line and sometimes slightly behind the singer. The harmonium is an instrument which has exerted a strong influence on concepts of pitch and thus on melodic presentation. It was an instrument patented by the French instrument maker Alexandre François Debain, in 1842 and it was widely disseminated by colonial powers in India and in Africa where it has played an important role in shaping local traditions (see Owen and Dick 1984, 131).

Score 2.3: "Phoulourie", Sundar Popo, transcribed extract

Score 2.4: "Indian Arrival", Sundar Popo, transcribed extract

Score 2.5: "We Voting UNC", Jairam Dindial, transcribed extract

In view of the harmonium's origins, the traditional chutney ensemble of *dhantal, dholak* and harmonium can be seen as a sound world of timbres which are respectively associated with the Caribbean, India and Europe. Musicians in Trinidad, as elsewhere, may have used musical instruments in ways which sound distinctive. Instrumental timbre, however, and the fixing of pitch according to the principles of diatonicism, which an instrument like the harmonium encourages, provide evidence of musical interactions between musical traditions, from the sounds themselves.

One further point about the harmonium can be made here. Its role in the performance of chutney is primarily melodic. It is not used to provide chordal harmony. But diatonic harmony, nevertheless, is also a feature of contemporary chutney. The harmonic structure of the verses of Terry Gajraj's "Guyana Baboo", for example, follows a standard I, IV, V pattern (see the extract from the rehearsal score, Score 2.6).

Score 2.6: "Guyana Baboo", Terry Gajraj, rehearsal score (reproduced with permission)

## TEXT

Chutney song texts deal with diverse themes: historical, social, topical, ribald and individual experience. A more thorough discussion of song texts will be pursued later in relation to the articulation of identity and in analysis of the political and cultural subtexts of song performance. In this section I shall discuss chutney song texts within the framework of Indian models.

Terry Gajraj sings about the Guyana Baboo, a song which relates his experiences: "Me come from de country they call Guyana, land of de bauxite, de rice and sugar." The "Baboo" appears in a song text heard by Captain Angel in Calcutta during the 1870s. Like Terry Gajraj's version, this song text deals with everyday experiences. In this example, these are the everyday experiences of a "Bengali Baboo" who sold wares in the cosmopolitan Radah Bazaar. It is a text that portrays interactions with the colonial authorities and contains references to crossing the *kala pani* (the black water). This crossing highlights the perception of wealth that can be gained and brought to India. It tells a story – fulfilling Sundar Popo's requirements for a song. This is the text as related by W. H. Angel (translations his):

"The Bengalee Baboo"

(1)
I very good Bengalee Baboo,
In Calcutta a long time e-stop;
Ram Jam Tundah Ghose my name;
In Radah Bazaar I keep it e-shop
Very good Hindoo, smoke my hookah (native pipe)
Eat my dhall-bat every day; (pan-cake)
Night time come, make plenty poojah, (fun)
Hear Nauch-wallah on tom-tom play. (dancing girls)

*Chorus*

Kautch-per-wanee, good time coming; (never mind)
Sing Britannia rules the wave,
Jolly good-e-fellow, go home in the morning –
Baboo how he can make slaves.

(2)

Sub Sahab logue, come my shop look now (stop sir)
Very good thing got, you shall see.
Not money want-it, give long credit,
Then sahab pay me plenty rupee,
Come inside . . . I very poor man, Sahab;
Something buy from me, I pray –
Bito – tell you what thing got now, (sit down)
I sell 'you' very cheap to-day.

*Chorus*

. . . . . . . . . . . .

(5)

Bye and bye make very long journey,
Cross Kalla-panee I shall go, (black water)
In Balattee country travel,
There I make one very big show,
Everybody give nice presents, read big books.
Then long time think;
Little time make good civil servant,
Eat beef-steak, and simpkin drink. (champagne)

*Chorus*

(6)

I then come back to Calcutta,
Not keep shop . . . how then can do?
Famine relief . . . give five rupees . . . then,
Everybody say . . . what kind Hindoo!
(Complete text in Ramchand and Samaroo 1995: 45–46.)

The "baboo", as in this example, was often the protagonist of
nineteenth century texts produced in Calcutta. Terry Gajraj's song about
the Guyanese baboo can be seen as stemming from this tradition. An
honorific term or a term of respect initially, the "baboo" also became an
expression of ridicule denoting Calcutta's nouveaux riches. This kind of
baboo was the pampered son who "having inherited his father's wealth
dissipates it on drinking, whoring and other amusements with a host of
sycophants" (Banerjee 1989, 180). Amongst his other vices are

"attending musical rehearsals" and "listening to songs" according to an early farcical account (Banerjee 1989, 180).

Sometimes the emphasis of a chutney song text is not on its narrative qualities. If Sundar Popo stressed that the interpretation of a song text is undertaken by the listener, he was also aware that some song texts will be interpreted in certain ways. Apparently innocuous words, "Phoulourie bina chutney, kaisay banee" (phoulourie without chutney, that's all that I'm preparing) carry double meanings which are understood by the audience. These double meanings add to the controversies that surround the performance of chutney. "Phoulourie without chutney, that's all that I'm preparing" can be read as sex without the spice, that's all you'll get. The song text is therefore interpreted as being "rude". Since these kinds of double meanings are found in calypso song texts, too, they contribute to comparisons made between chutney and calypso. These interpretations of song texts have a bearing on the dance style of chutney. In addition to the public spaces in which it is displayed, the choreography of chutney dance is unacceptable to some observers because the song text offers such alternative readings. Dance movements are interpreted according to implicit understandings of song texts. These textual aspects are taken into account, then, in discussions concerning the private/public boundaries of chutney performance.

Many of those who object to the public performance of chutney in Trinidad do so on the basis that the form is a degradation of Indian culture and chutney is frequently compared to calypso to make the point that it is not "properly" Indian. Yet chutney can be compared, in this respect, to Indian models, particularly to some nineteenth century traditions prominent in the city (Calcutta) which was the location of one of the main "coolie depots" from where Indian migrants to the Caribbean began their journeys.

The controversies surrounding textual and dance aspects of chutney and arguments that the use of overt eroticism is a degradation of "Indian" culture are reminiscent of the response of Calcutta's elite to nineteenth century urban folk expressions. A new generation of Bengalis in Calcutta, who had been educated under a colonial system, sought to disassociate themselves from urban expressions which had been popular with all sectors of the city's population. The *jatra*, a folk theatrical form, was one of those expressions which was criticized for defiling Hindu divinities and degrading them in the eyes of the English. Like chutney, the *jatra* had its origins in ritual songs and dances performed as part of religious festivals in villages. Drums and *tanpura* [long necked plucked drone lute] were the instruments used, but by the end of the nineteenth century, Western instruments like the harmonium and clarinet formed part of the *jatra* orchestra. Gopal Udey (1817–57) was one of the leading proponents of the *jatra* and he introduced a type of dancing, *khemta*, which was characterized by its erotic overtones and suggestive movements. It was imitated by many dance troupes. Banerjee suggests that the "ribaldry and sexual jokes in the *jatras* were often an expression of the common man's desire to thumb his nose at the self-restraints and sanctimonious platitudes of the religious elders of society" and that the audience "were not looking surreptitiously for lewd kicks, but were used [from traditional folk culture] to watching such spectacles and listening to such bawdy exchanges as innocent entertainment (1989, 140–41). The urban "folk" may well have regarded these entertainments as innocent, but there were other inhabitants of the city who did not.

In 1873 a Society for the Suppression of Public Obscenity was established. The writer and editor of the newspaper, *Bangadarshan*, Bankim Chandra Chattopadhyay, offered his support, writing: "It would not be an exaggeration to say that obscenity is the national vice of the Bengalis. Those who may consider this to be an exaggeration, should merely think of Bengali jokes, Bengali abuses, the wranglings among Bengali women of the lower orders, and Bengali *jatra*" (cited in Banerjee 1989, 184). The public performance of *jatra* was criticized in terms which match criticisms of chutney: "Who that has any pretension to a polite taste will not be disgusted with the vulgar mode of dancing with which our play commences; and who that has any moral tendency will not censure the immorality of the pieces that are performed?" wrote a commentator in a letter to the *Morning Chronicle* (January 1855, cited in Banerjee 1989, 159). These responses to urban folk forms in Calcutta are echoed in contemporary contexts in Trinidad in relation to chutney as we shall see in chapter 4.

The aspect of repartee between singers is also found in Indian and Caribbean contexts. Urban folk singers in Calcutta engaged in poetic duels that became a popular form of entertainment during the eighteenth century (Banerjee 1989, 82). The calypsonian model of exchanging verbal insults and satirical comments, that famous Trinidad picong, had an Indian counterpart. Chutney singers, then, can be seen as drawing on both models of commentary and criticism. Sonny Mann gained his title of Chutney Monarch (1995) singing "Loota La" which was a song full of innuendo but with nothing stated explicitly about a woman rolling drunk and dancing. His song was not understood initially by everybody because he sang in Bhojpuri. As the meaning of the song became more generally known it sparked controversy. It was controversial because the drunk, dancing woman was described as *bhowji* (sister-in-law) and thus seemed to indicate a lack of respect for the social and gender relations observed by Indian-Caribbean people. In the song the singer relates that his brother is working very hard in the fields. His brother's wife goes to bathe in the back of the house and "invites" her brother-in-law to "roll" with her:

*Daroo peeke bhowji khub loota la*
*bhaiya leke gari khub kamkarela*
*hamare bhaiya bhowji khub gawela*
*hamare bhaiya na samjhela*
*leke sabun bhowji khub lagawela* . . .

*bhowji* drank wine, tumbling very much
brother took a van, working very hard
our brother *bhowji* singing very much
our brother does not understand
took soap, *bhowji* uses very much . . .

The singer sings in the chorus "*loota bhowji, khub loota la*" (let us roll sister-in-law, with great gusto let us roll – literally "tumble very much"). In response, Sundar Popo entered the fray (seizing an opportunity for topical commentary) and released a song, "Cold Water" (1996), in which he sings: "Sonny Mann, cool yourself with cold water, you lotaying your *bhowji* and not your brother." Popo expressed the sentiments of many listeners in chastizing Sonny Mann for singing about a sister-in-law in such a manner. Amina Ramsaran's song, "Eh Bhaiya Bhowji" can also be interpreted in relation to Sonny Mann's "Loota La". Ramsaran sings about the brother-in-law washing dishes and preparing food for his sister-in-law. Without the sister-in-law, the brother would not be able to live (*bhowji bina bhaiya na janae rahe*), and would be crying at home (*bhowji na rahe bhaiya gharawan me roee*). If Sonny Mann's text is an attack on the sister-in-law, Amina Ramsaran ridicules the brother-in-law.

Sonny Mann's and Amina Ramsaran's texts display a freedom in commenting on kinship relations that would be less acceptable in ordinary discourse. Heeralal Rampartap displayed a similar freedom in commenting on audience reactions to chutney. His song, "Chutney Possy" (1995), was very popular although he described his audience as consisting of young girls behaving in ways that provoke strong criticism: dancing to the drum and drinking rum. This song was not met with the same kind of criticism levelled at "Loota La", perhaps because it depicts the behaviour of a crowd of (unidentified) chutney participants rather than a close kin like the sister-in-law.

**Heeralal Rampartap (extract, text transcribed from MC Records cassette MC0013, 1995)**

"Chutney Possy"

I on the stage and I singing my song,
if you see them young girls they wining to the drum.
It's the chutney possy [crowd],
the chutney possy dancing and singing along.
If you hear the talk all over the town,
it's the chutney possy following the wonderboy around.
Look how my possy they drinking their rum,
they're hearing my song and dancing to the drum.

Like Sonny Mann's "Loota La", another song which caused controversy because of its text was Chris Garcia's "Chutney Bacchanal" (chutney soca song, 1996). The controversy surrounded what were said to be Hindi swear words (chorus 1) but which the singer claimed were simply nonsense words. The song text also falls into the category of songs which are criticized for their negative depictions of women, and for repetitive instructions to the audience to "wine" (gyrate), "go down" and "come up". Because of its popularity, the text of Chris Garcia's chutney soca song, "Chutney Bacchanal" was reproduced in newspapers and had been memorized by many listeners:

"Chutney Bacchanal"

(1)
A woman come down from India,
tell me she love up the soca,

want to sing a verse in Hindi,
so she grab hold of my guitar
then start to deliver
and this is what it sound like,
jamming on me all night
this is what it sounds like to me.

*Chorus 1*

*chadey burcuhchun dey*
*burgayjardey*
*burgungee*
*brickchadey*
*burkayjonkay*
*lika dukalikynani*
*jukalikynani*
*burgayjunggayda*
*jukalikynani.*

*Chorus 2*

Chutney bacchanal
chutney carnival
chutney bacchanal
chutney, chutney, chutney, chutney
oh lord, oy, oy
chutney, chutney, chutney bacchanal.

(2)
Body start to shiver
my body start to quiver
just vibing on this new wave chutney,
the woman gone in a frenzy
wailing up she body
and I and all in sweet ecstasy.
This is what it sound like
jamming on me all night
this is what it sound like to me

*Choruses 1 and 2*

Chutney bacchanal, oh, oh
come with it gyul [girl]
chutney bacchanal, oh, oh
chutney bacchanal
chutney bacchanal, oh, oh
fire the water
fire the water
come.

(3)
Some people start to jump up,
who was sitting get up,
chutney madness on a rampage.
A Chinee man, he was passing
chutney send he insane
if you see the man wine on stage.
This is what it sound like
jamming on me all night
this is what it sound like to me.

(*Choruses 1 and 2*

Oh, oyo
oh, everybody come come
oh, one hand on the waist, one hand in the air
oh, wine, wine, wine, wine
oh, go down, go down, go down, go down, go down
oh, come up, come up, come up, come up, come up
oh, fire the water, fire the water
oh, chutney bacchanal,
chutney bacchanal.

Issues about meanings and the ways in which song texts are interpreted and represented are apparent, too, in Grierson's work. Grierson
was more interested in textual matters than in other musical aspects of
Bihari and Bhojpuri folk song traditions. In contrast to his statement that
he knew of no new tunes, he pointed out changes in song texts. Where
he was concerned with recording a fixed text, "native" commentators

were not averse, in contrast, to changing the text. Seeking to avoid textual changes, as he specified in the introduction to his 1884 paper, his collection of texts was made with the assistance of Shiv Nandan Laal Raay, on whom he seems to have relied quite extensively:

> The following songs are a portion of those collected by me last hot weather, when acting as Magistrate of Patna. They were written down for me in the heart of Bihar by Babu Shiv Nandan Laal Raay, Deputy Magistrate, a gentleman born and bred in the neighbourhood of Ara (Arrah), who takes a most lively interest in his own beautiful native language. I have printed them exactly as they have been taken from the mouths of the reciters, a few obvious slips of the pen being alone corrected. I have allowed no theories of my own to interfere with the text obtained, and I have religiously abstained from consulting even competent native scholars as to probable or possible emendations. Natives in such cases are, as is well known, only too ready to invent readings which have never existed. They have no reverence whatever for the words or matter of songs in the vernacular, and feel themselves justified in making any alterations or additions on the spur of the moment, which may seem required by the metre, or more adapted to their present temperament. (1884, 196)

Although Grierson states at the outset that the song texts were collected by him and that they were notated exactly as recited without the addition of either his own commentary or the "invented readings" of native scholars, it turns out that the role of his assistant was far more significant in this process of collecting folklore than is at first apparent. As we read further we find out that, in fact, Grierson was not present when the song texts were recited:

> the great preservers of these songs are the women of all classes, and it is therefore impossible for a European to obtain them direct from their storekeepers. I am hence doubly indebted to Babu Shiv Nandan Laal Raay, who has given me these songs exactly as they have been taken down from the mouths of ladies in Shahabad. (Grierson 1884, 196)

Grierson's critique of this methodological approach is directed not at the process of collection and on the representation of a personally undertaken project but on the content of some of the texts:

> I have already stated that these songs are printed ipsissmis verbis, as they were recited by women of the Bhojpuri tract. This has its advantages, but it must be

confessed, it also has disadvantages. The uneducated, and especially women, have a great reverence for the unintelligible . . . Hence many an obscure word is retained simply because it is not understood, and finally after generations of ignorant attrition becomes a sound and nothing more, having no meaning in itself, but interesting simply from its unintelligibility. (Grierson 1884, 198)

A more recent study of the Bhojpuri-speaking area (Henry 1976, 58) likewise indicates that once enough of the sense of the words is understood, most listeners are satisfied without knowing the meaning of the whole song text.

If Bhojpuri is not understood by all the audience in the Caribbean context, it seems that neither were all of the words used in nineteenth century Bihari and Bhojpuri folk songs. In the contemporary north Indian village context, too, an understanding of the complete text is not necessary. The sound of the word can be retained for its intrinsic properties and association with the past rather than its meaning. Indeed, language educationalists in Trinidad emphasize the learning of Hindi nowadays instead of the more common language, Bhojpuri, of their Indian ancestors. The Bhojpuri song text in Trinidad assumes, in part, a symbolic importance: the language of some of the ancestors. Myers reports that in Felicity, a village in North Trinidad,

Indian music is different things to different people. For the younger generation it refers especially to Indian film songs, for the older to the traditional Bhojpuri folk songs, and for practically everybody to temple songs, such as bhajan and kirtan. For all, it means a repertory with texts in an Indian language. (1993a, 235)

Despite the emphasis on language, many contemporary chutney song texts are in English with just a few Bhojpuri or Hindi words added. Sometimes a Bhojpuri or Hindi text intermingles with its English translation. The choice of language (English) is significant for two main reasons: it is the language of today's Indian-Trinidadian population, and Trinidadians from a non-Indian background find chutney more accessible than, for example, Indian religious songs. Note should be made here of the difficulties surrounding the issue of language and of the use of Bhojpuri and Hindi. Singers often refer to their use of Hindi when in fact they sing in Bhojpuri. While some regard Bhojpuri as a language separate from Hindi, others regard it as a Hindi dialect. In Trinidad, matters are further complicated. Bhojpuri may have been the main language of the indentured labourers, however, school children in Trinidad today have opportunities to study Hindi, rather than Bhojpuri. Moreover, one of the dialects from Lucknow, Avadhi (spoken in Avadh) can still be heard in areas of south Trinidad (like Penal). Avadhi is close to Bhojpuri. In fact, chutney song texts often include a mixture of Bhojpuri, Avadhi, Hindi and also Urdu.

## STRUCTURE

The overall structure of many chutney songs is that of the verse and chorus format. The rhythmic structure is simple. The *taal* (cycle of beats) is usually *kaherwa* (simple quadruple time, 4/4). Adesh identifies *kaherwa taal* as the dominant *taal* of light (for example, film) and folk music (in Myers 1984, 383). The metric structure tends to be syllabic and settings can be closely related to speech rhythms. With regard to melodic structure, a song can consist of a few melodic "cells" which are repeated.

All of these structural features: verse and chorus format, repetition, the organization of rhythmic stresses in a simple quadruple time, and a syllabic metric structure can be observed in Anand Yankaran's song, "Guyana Kay Dulahin" (Score 2.7, see next page).

As can be seen from my transcription of this song (melody only), the melodic cells of the chorus can be depicted diagrammatically as appearing in the following format (where A, B and C represent different melodic statements):

*Chorus: melodic cells and pitch range*

A–8 bars where the first 4 bars of this cell are repeated (text: "Oh Guyana kay dulahin, come to Trinidad, I want to be your dulaha"). The pitch range is between the interval of a seventh;

B–4 bars (text: "Oh Guyana kay dulahin, come to Trinidad, I really love you and that's the reason why"). The pitch range is between the interval of a fifth;

C–4 bars where the first two bars of this cell are repeated (text: "Guyana kay dulahin, come to Trinidad"). The pitch range is between the interval of a fourth.

*Score 2.7: "Guyana Kay Dulahin", Anand Yankaran, transcribed extract*

Two melodic cells appear in the verses. The melodic cell of the first verse is four bars in length, where the first two bars are repeated, and the second cell is two bars long.

The verse and chorus structural format can be outlined as:

short instrumental introduction;
chorus + melodic cell A of the chorus repeated;
verse 1 (different text) and chorus;
instrumental interlude;
verse 2 (different text) and chorus;
verse 3 (as transcribed in Score 2.7) and chorus;

instrumental interlude (as before);

verse 4 (different text) and chorus;

verse 5 (different text) and chorus.

## INSTRUMENTATION

While electronic instruments, programmed drum machines and brass instruments like the saxophone and trumpet contribute to the instrumental timbre of chutney soca, the instruments which are identified as being essential to the chutney sound are the *dhantal, dholak* and harmonium. The instrumentation of a traditional chutney song consists only of voice, *dhantal, dholak* and harmonium. The *dhantal* will be investigated further because it is represented as being a particularly Indian-Caribbean instrument.

### The *Dhantal* (or *Dandtal*): An Indian-Caribbean Percussion Idiophone Reconsidered

The complete entry under *dandtal* in the *New Grove Dictionary of Musical Instruments* reads as follows: "(Hindi: 'stick percussion'). A percussion idiophone of north Indian origin, played in Trinidad and Surinam. It consists of an iron rod, about one metre long, which is struck with a horseshoe shaped beater. The left hand is used to damp the rod" (Brandily 1984, 541). This entry presents an uncomplicated view of the instrument. The details, however, need some clarification, particularly with regard to the origin of the *dandtal*. If the instrument originates from north India, is it played there too? If not, how can its presence in the Caribbean be explained? The description in this dictionary is contested by Caribbean commentators.

We can note first, that although the entry in the *Grove Dictionary* only locates the use of the *dandtal* in Trinidad and Suriname, the instrument is played in Guyana too and it is associated with Indian-Caribbean populations generally. In Trinidad, the instrument is more commonly known as the *dhantal*. As described in the *Grove Dictionary*, this instrument is an iron, or sometimes a steel rod which is struck by a horseshoe-shaped beater. The top of the iron rod, however, is tapered to a fine point to allow greater resonance and the end is shaped into a circle which rests on the ground, table, or other surface when it is played. Its length is around a metre, as the *Grove Dictionary* states, but this varies depending on materials available at the time of production (see Photo 2). The *dhantal* is usually made by the player for personal use but can also be commissioned via *puja* shops which sell articles associated with religious ceremonies. Before it is ready to be played, the rod must be sanded with sandpaper.

Caribbean commentators have suggested that the instrument is not found in India (although similar percussion instruments are). Theories concerning its origin include the view that the instrument was "invented" by Indian labourers who began to use rods from estate oxen or horse carts as percussion instruments on the Caribbean sugar plantations. The beater for the rod, according to this origin theory, was literally the horseshoe, a shape that has been retained in contemporary contexts. In this view the origin of the *dhantal* is bound up with experiences of the sugar plantation around which the labourers' lives revolved. Kurup's sesquicentenary review essay includes a photograph of oxen yoked together. The caption informs the reader that the yoke and shaft of the oxen cart "are joined by a steel pin which became an integral part of the Indian musical ensemble in Trinidad" (Kurup 1995, 40). This is a theory, then, which has been accepted as historical fact in an important celebratory volume of Indian-Caribbean experiences. In another theory of the *dhantal*'s origin, performance context is stressed. The steel rod which was used to hold large cooking pots over the fireplace is seen as eventually being struck as another percussion instrument during festive occasions. This is an alternative theory of the instrument's origin which has been posited by the dancer, Satnarine Balkaransingh, who doubts that indentured labourers would have had the time or opportunity to engage in much musical activity while working on the plantation. He suggests that just as the *lota* (bronze goblet) is struck with spoons nowadays to provide another "instrument" played at wedding celebrations, the *dhantal* could have been an adaptation of an ordinary cooking implement (personal interview, July 1996).[2] In reclaiming an "Indian" history, another theory is that the *dhantal* is an ancient Indian instrument which has been held in the biogenetic memory of Indian-Caribbean populations. There seems to be no documentation which proves conclusively whether the first migrants brought the *dhantal* with them, or whether they and their descendents only started to play this instrument in the Caribbean. There is, however, an early reference to *dhantal* in Mahabir's (1985) compilation of the recorded reminiscences of first generation Indian migrants to Trinidad. Fazal says (using language dated to around 1910):

when cutting cane how e [he] go sing
when go home
bathe an ting [and thing]
eat an ting
den [then] could sing.

Group have drum an ting
sitar
majeera [manjeera]
sarangi
dey bin have [they had]
dem [them] bring from India
e [he] no have no dantal
e [he] no have no organ.
    (in Mahabir 1985, 58)

According to Fazal's testimony, instruments which originated from India and were played in Trinidad included drums, *sitar* (I shall return to this in chapter five), *ma[n]jeera* and *sarangi*, but neither the *dhantal* nor the organ (harmonium) were played by sugar cane workers with whom he came into contact. Was the *dhantal* a later adaptation? There are some similar north Indian models and the name given to the instrument is a literal term: *dandtal* (stick percussion; *danda* – stick, *taal* – act of striking from which the sense of rhythmic cycle may originate). Marcus (1992, 104) notes, for example, that the instruments played in the performance of the north Indian folk music, *biraha* (a narrative, Banaras-based Bhojpuri genre which also survives in Trinidad), are metallic idiophone instruments called *kartal* (wooden clappers which may have jingles), *dholak* and harmonium. These are the instrumental timbres found in chutney.

The *Grove Dictionary* entry for *kartal* describes the instrument denoted as pairs of wooden clappers which may have jingles. In Bihar the instrument is *danda* (a name very close to *dhantal*), a simple wooden clapper, while in Bengal and Orissa it is a pair of medium-sized bell-metal cymbals which are widely used in religious music (Dick 1984, 361–62). Henry (1976) also describes north Indian genres which resemble chutney in terms of instrumental timbre, as well as performance context. He too writes about *viraha* (Marcus's *biraha*). These are songs performed by a group of men at weddings. The instruments which accompany are the *dholak* and a metallophone consisting of two iron rods. Whereas the *dhantal* is played using both hands, Henry writes that both the iron rods of the metallophone instrument used in *viraha* are held loosely and clanged together in one hand.

*Biraha* is also found in Trinidad. Ramnath writes about the genre as one which has various styles. It is usually "composed on the spot" (improvised), accompanied by drums called *naggara* [small kettledrum] and the singers may also dance. The songs are usually performed at weddings (Ramnath n.d., 109). A more recent reference to *biraha* is an article about the genre in Trinidad in the newspaper, *Sunday Express* (5 May 1996, 4). Praimsingh, the record retailer who has plans to promote this genre, is quoted as saying that "the artform has never been featured prominently". The author of the article, Essiba Small, characterizes *biraha* as having "an up-and-down intonation and songs can last as long as 15 minutes. Topics usually come from the *Ramayan* or the *Gita*."

Where chutney draws on an Indian heritage, it seems to be an amalgam of different north Indian folk traditions. Other genres found in the Bhojpuri-speaking area include *kaharava* songs which are characterized, according to Henry, by melodic simplicity, repetition and rhythmic timbres of drum and idiophone accompaniment. They too are performed at weddings. *Nauthaki* is a music and dance genre. Harmonium, *dholak* and singers provide music for a female-impersonating dancer (Henry 1976, 59–60). This genre, the *nautch* (the same variant of the term is used by Banerjee 1989), was described by Satnarine Balkaransingh who remembered seeing the dance as a young child. He said that male dancers who performed the *nautch* were allowed to participate in women's private performance spheres. The men's dancing style was "inelegant" (personal interview, July 1996).

## Playing the Dhantal

The iron steel rod is loosely supported by the left hand. By closing the left hand, a player damps the resonance of the rod as it is struck. The rod is alternately dampened and allowed to resonate by releasing the left hand's grip. This action allows two distinct timbres to be obtained. Volume is controlled either by beating the rod nearer to the top (softer dynamic) or the end (louder). The technique of striking the rod with the horseshoe-shaped beater is to rotate the right wrist in a semicircular movement so that the beater is struck on both sides. Score 2.8 shows rhythmic patterns typically played on the *dhantal.*

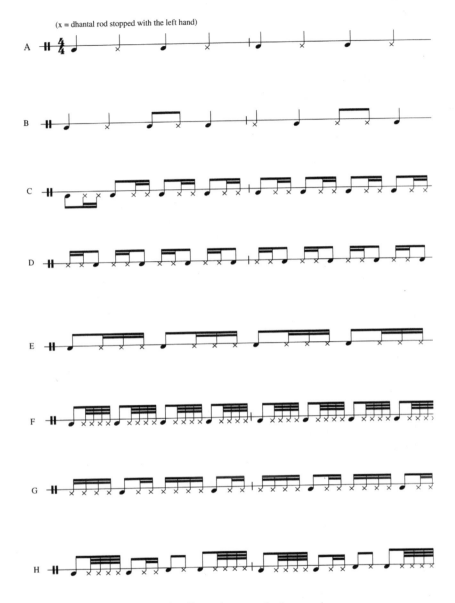

*Score 2.8: Rhythms played on the* dhantal, *transcribed examples*

## Performance Contexts

The *dhantal*, an instrument which is easily manufactured and played, appears in diverse performance contexts: in the performance of religious songs, rum-shop songs, wedding celebration songs, chutney and calypso.

Although tempo varies, the same rhythmic patterns transcribed in Score 2.8 are used in these different genres. In chutney, the most common rhythmic patterns are those of Scores 2.8(c) and 2.8(d), played at a fast tempo. The player of the *dhantal* follows the lead of a singer in a performance ensemble but chooses which rhythmic patterns to play.

Although the vocal part is of prime importance, it is the *dhantal*, together with the *dholak* and the harmonium, which have become symbols of "Indianness" in Indian-Caribbean music. This is partly due to its widespread use in the performance of most contemporary Indian-Caribbean musical genres. Even if the genre is not identified as an "Indian-Caribbean" one, the instrumentation may denote a particular ethnic and cultural identity. Thus, the Guyanese singer, Terry Gajraj, claimed that he was producing Indian-Caribbean versions of old calypso favourites on the basis that he was adding *dhantal*, *dholak* and harmonium to the instrumental texture (personal interview, May 1996).[3]

Reasons why the *dhantal* has come to play such an important musical and symbolic role in the expression of Indian-Caribbean identity have been indicated in this book by examining the emergence of the instrument in particular historical and geographic contexts. Yet, rather than provide answers, the examination of the *dhantal* in this chapter has raised more questions. Despite the description found in the *Grove Dictionary*, of the *dhantal* as an instrument which originated in one part of the world but is played in another, its origin, as discussed here, remains something of a mystery. There are Indian models, but whatever its origin, it is clear that the importance of the *dhantal* is in the Caribbean, not in the Indian, context.

## TRANSMITTING THE TRADITION

"How did you become a musician?" I asked James Ramsawak (a musician and teacher who was born in Trinidad in 1917).

"My father was a singer and a *dholak* drummer," he replied.

I learnt to sing because he was a drummer playing for singers and I picked it up by listening. I started to sing when I was twelve years old, singing the women's songs. Because I was little I sang and played the harmonium for the women. Long ago you couldn't get men playing for the women – them women dancing, they wining like hell. When I became a young man I branched off to English songs – which I learnt from records. Then a star came from India: Bhavaria. He had a show in the Globe Theatre in San Fernando. When I sat down and listened to him singing Indian songs I thought, "But this thing has a great future, man, I will pick it up." And I started to sing Indian songs. The manager of the theatre invited me to have an evening of fete [go to a party] with him [Bhavaria] because I was quite well-known. Bhavaria said, "Sing something." I said "I can't sing Indian songs." "Well sing what you can," he told me, so I sang an Elvis [Presley] song for him. [I think that Ramsawak's memory is a bit confused here for he is describing a period, the late 1930s, before the advent of Elvis Presley.] When he heard my voice he told me that I was good and asked why I didn't learn to sing Indian songs. I said, "I haven't got anybody to teach me." "You can learn your-self, get some records. I'll give a competition – learn one song," he told me. He organized a competition and I learnt a classical Indian song and came second. From then on I sang Indian songs. (personal interview, 30 July 1996)[4]

I have chosen James Ramsawak as an example here because of his involvement with music since the early twentieth century. By 1936, at the age of nineteen when he attended Bhavaria's performance, he was already an established local musician. During the 1940s, he led a group of eight singers, managed by Moean Mohammed, on a tour to Surinam and Guyana: "We were the first Indian singers who left these shores to go to Surinam," he said (personal interview, 1996). Such tours must have contributed to the exchange of musical ideas between Indian-Caribbean musicians and audiences. James Ramsawak has also played an important role with regard to chutney, for many of the currently acclaimed singers studied with him. He has composed songs for his students: singers like Sundar Popo, Drupatee Ramgoonai and Lilly Ramcharan, and for competitions, including *Mastana Bahar*.

Evident from Ramsawak's statement is that he learnt music following the principles of oral transmission. But different sources provided the musical models and repertoire which he studied. He began by learning from the environment of the family and from participating in local musical events such as the wedding ceremonies. At these ceremonies he learnt a repertoire of women's songs which he accompanied on the harmonium. Later, he turned to a repertoire of Anglo-American popular songs which he heard on records. Following his participation in the competition he described, his major work has been with the performance of Indian songs and the composition of "local Indian" music. He was one of the first male musicians, according to his own testimony, to encourage the public performance of women's songs and to regard that repertoire as one which could also be performed by men.

Statements about composing chutney songs demonstrate the difficulties musicians (and analysts alike) face in talking about creative processes. Ramsawak described the process of composing the song, "The New Dawn", written for the 1995 Indian Arrival Day celebrations. Like Sundar Popo, he expressed a clear sense of material "belonging" to him. Lilly Ramcharan performed the song on radio, but Ramsawak had otherwise refused to "give" the song to other performers or promoters. He did, however, give an extract of the song to me for this project, and he described the song in terms of textual content and musical style. The song begins in a "classical calypso style" and then "calypso is mixed with Indian tunes – with chutney and qawwali". The text is mostly in English but the first verse is in Bhojpuri (what he described as Hindi). The musical styles which he incorporates in the song are in keeping with the text and with processes of musical change in new contexts. This is the extract of the text:

[Introduction]
In 1845 the British started their cunning drive,
sending the poor people of Hindustan in [to] this land
to slave for the Englishman.

(1)
*Jai Jai Trinbago mahaan*
*Aaj tay ray jiwan ka howe bihan*
*kya bunha nowjewan*
*tay ray jiwan ka howe bihan?*
(Long live great Trinidad and Tobago,
Today your life, what is it going to be tomorrow
What will the young people become,
your life, what is it going to be tomorrow?)

Ramsawak, having read some literature on the theory and philosophy of Indian music, believes that music comes from the ether (personal interview, 1996). Similarly, the singer Cecil Fonrose explained,

Sometimes something come[s] into your mind and you want to sing a song about it. Sometimes I sing in English and I mix English with Hindi. Sometimes when I want a new song, it mostly come[s] in Hindi. I don't know where and how it does come but I accept it. I never used to take copies [write it down]. (personal interview, 1996)[5]

Fonrose's explanation can be compared with Terry Gajraj's statement:

If I think and say, okay I want to write a song, I never do. It just comes. Like maybe I'm listening to another song or I'm reading something and there's an idea right there and I say, "Oh, I'll use that, I'll build a song around that." It just happens like that. (personal interview, 1996)

## Notated Scores, Recordings, Radio, Media

As with many other traditional musics, notated scores (provided, for example, by music arrangers for session musicians), sound recordings and media transmission (radio, television, newspapers and the like) play a significant role in the transmission of contemporary chutney. Although Cecil Fonrose talked about keeping his songs by memory and other singers talked about writing just the song text, many performers employ music arrangers to write down parts for instrumentalists, such as trumpeters and keyboard players, who collaborate with the singer in performance or in recording. Score 2.6 ("Guyana Baboo") is one such notated score. It was produced by a music arranger for rehearsal and performance purposes. Of course, the provision and use of these notated scores is one way of transmitting the chutney tradition which departs from the model of oral transmission. As such it is not unlike contemporary folk music forms in other geographic contexts.

Mention must be made here of Moean Mohammed who played an important role in transmitting Indian-Caribbean music through organizing concert tours, through a radio programme which he began presenting in 1947, and in setting up the televised talent spotting competition, *Mastana Bahar*, in the 1960s. This competition has been an important forum for exhibiting Indian cultural revival performances. Talent scouts travel to different parts of the island highlighting the different kinds of activities that are taking place and prizes are given at the final competition. Manuel states that the brothers Sham and Moean Mohammed "correctly boast that they have played a significant role in the Indo-Trinidadian cultural revival, not only spreading awareness of Indian popular music and dance but, more importantly, inspiring a prodigious amount of local amateur creativity" (1997–98, 23). Around

eighty thousand people are estimated to have participated in the competition. Nowadays, local newspapers regularly feature articles on singers,
songs and performances, and advertisements for performance events and
competitions.

Malm and Wallis write that in the 1960s

the media had a tendency to avoid addressing the problems of the nation's
multi-ethnic music culture, preferring instead to stay safe with a mixture of
Anglo-American popular music and some Western art music. This, of course,
also reflected the conditions that had prevailed during the period of British colonialism. The colonial elite tended to consider music from Europe superior to
local kinds of music. (1992, 68)

Thus James Ramsawak's recorded output is small ("Hindi Kawali" and
"Dadha", Decca 16505 and 16503, 1940) and he remembers that "in those
days the making of records was very rare" (personal interview, 1996).

If the music transmitted by the media in Trinidad was largely Anglo-
American during the 1960s, people still recall important Indian-
Caribbean contributions which shaped musical activity at the time. The
occasional Indian-Caribbean songs which were heard on the radio or on a
jukebox contributed to a general repertoire and to the transmission of
chutney-type songs. The following is a testimony in which the narrator is
recollecting musical memories from a village during the 1960s and 1970s:

One of the [chutney] songs that really became popular, although it was rude and
people found it unacceptable, was "Roza Roza Dulahin" [enjoy yourself, enjoy
yourself bride]. Deep down a lot of people really enjoyed the song because it was
something new and it was broadcast on the radio. It was played on the radio regularly. It wasn't a hush-hush song which people, like ladies singing on a Friday
night for a wedding, only used to sing in private . . . People started becoming
more and more bold, especially the men. They used to sing during Farewell
nights for example during the orchestral interval. If they had an opportunity
they used to get up and sing. Some of them were really good, some were really
rude. They sang on their own. By that stage, late at night, most of them were
drunk and when you're drunk and you sing it sounds good. But people used to
listen and laugh and enjoy it. I think it went on from there – people got more
bold. One of the popular songs was this song [roza roza dulahin] which Bhadase
Maraj [a self-made millionaire who merged two Hindu organizations in
Trinidad to form the group known as the *Sanatan Dharma Maha Sabha*]

protested against. After a while the song was withdrawn but people got the taste for chutney. I remember as kids we used to sing it and our mothers telling us to shut up, we didn't know what we were singing. (Robin Ramsaran, personal interview, 1997)[6]

The importance of radio as a medium for the transmission of this song is paralleled by the role that radio and commercial recordings play today in gaining audiences for chutney. Malm and Wallis continue their analysis of media transmission of music in Trinidad as follows:

one of the more notable developments during the past two decades has been a gradual increase in the share of Trinidadian music in the total media output. This is particularly true of the music for the carnival season: calypso, steelband, etc. But the same also applies to other kinds of music such as the Christmas parang music, forms which are known in Trinidad as East Indian music, choral music based on local folk songs, etc. (1992, 68)

Chutney has been recorded by companies like JMC (Jamaican Music Connection, otherwise known as Jamaica Me Crazy, based in New York) and local promoters. One promoter of chutney in Trinidad is Praimsingh who runs a record shop in Chaguanas. His family has been involved with

Photo 5: The promoter, Praimsingh, in his shop with some examples of his recording production

the music retail business for three generations. His grandfather was from Bihar. He set up the record retail business in Trinidad and sold records which he imported from India. Praimsingh has recently begun to record chutney singers and regards himself as one of the main promoters of Indian-Caribbean music. As well as recordings of chutney singers (including Amina Ramsaran, Suresh Maharaj, Jairam Dindial), he has recorded *tassa* groups, *chowtal* (songs sung in praise of Krishna) and religious music – *bhajans* (personal interview, 6 July 1996).[7]

These recordings will play a central role in the provision of sound documents of current musical activity for the future. More immediately, the recordings influence the ways in which chutney is transmitted by making the tradition accessible to diverse audiences and enabling musicians to get and exchange musical ideas from performances that can be repeated at will.

# Chapter 3

# Chutney as an Expression of Indian-Caribbean Identity

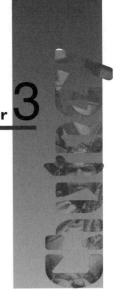

For some commentators, chutney is simply good party music. Some dislike chutney because it is music with too much "wining" (gyrating) and "jamming" (partying). In this chapter I shall interpret chutney shows as cultural performances which comment (through song texts in particular) on the experiences of a diasporic people for whom the diasporic context (the Caribbean) has become the new homeland.

As a tradition which has developed in a diasporic context, chutney emerges not as an Indian but as a specifically Indian-Caribbean form of expression.[1] Performances of chutney create a sense of relatedness for performers and audiences, and affirm a specific ethnic and cultural identity. These performances have contributed to debates over national culture. Stuempfle notes that Caribbean societies, as places where people have roots elsewhere, necessitate revising concepts of culture as self-contained. While Trinidad is culturally diverse, people are aware nevertheless to varying degrees of "distinctively local practices". These form the basis for building a sense of national identity, but since there is no "single conception of this identity . . . debate rages over what constitutes the national culture" (1995, 10).

Similarly, there is no single conception of an Indian-Caribbean identity and the reception to chutney and to its place in national culture has been varied. I am not arguing therefore that chutney is the musical expression of a unified community, but I do suggest that it plays a significant role in debates and expressions of an Indian-Caribbean identity in broad terms.

Music can be interpreted in diverse and even contrasting ways, which makes it a potentially powerful area of discussion in public debate. Although research on chutney has barely begun, all kinds of claims are already being made for it. In surveying press reports on the Trinidad Carnival, February of 1996, it is clear that chutney means different things to different people. One view is that it is an "Indian" tradition, and that recent chutney songs give the first indications of a movement of a people "to lay claim as authentic Indians in Trinidad and Tobago" (Ken Parmasad, cited in Alexander 1996, 2). Another view is that it is not quite Indian and does not reveal the real musical wealth of India's musical traditions which are also available to Indians in the Caribbean (Ravi-Ji 1996, 13). While these offer different perspectives, chutney's emergence as a popular genre is interlinked in these approaches with issues of the place, status and changing roles of Indians in the Caribbean. In discussions of these issues, the emphasis has been placed on "ethnicity" and "culture".

A concern with ethnicity forms part of the complex relations that exist between different ethnic groups in Trinidad. The song text, particularly the calypso text as a well-established form of social commentary, has been a medium for exploring these dynamics, characterized both by dissension and by solidarity (see Deosaran 1987). Discussions about the preservation and mixing of cultures in chutney have been fuelled by the incorporation of African-Caribbean musical elements, for example, calypso rhythms. Such musical interaction, and the debate it inspires, are of course central to the interpretation of chutney as an Indian-Caribbean tradition and throughout this study I draw attention to the mobility of "cultural elements". The focus here, however, will be on chutney as an expression of an Indian-Caribbean identity: an identity which is expressed in the song texts by references to cultural practices and objects, the experience of migration and kinship systems.

## CHUTNEY AND CARNIVAL

The search for parallel musical practices between Indian and Indian-Caribbean populations seems to point to performances of chutney in Trinidad as the preservation of tradition. These kinds of links with another homeland and with the past are obviously vital in reflecting on particular identities. Yet the tradition has changed. Chutney shows today usually feature a solo singer (male or female) with a backing band. They are held in formal performance contexts: in halls and theatres. In addition to the continued use of the *dholak*, the instrumentation often includes *dhantal*, guitars, keyboards and drum machines. Members of the audience, particularly women, invariably get up to dance at these shows. In short, changes lie in new conceptualizations and treatment of folksongs, so that this is now a musical repertory to which men can turn as well as women; in performance contexts, from the riverside as part of ritual to the stage as entertainment; and in the music itself, from the singing, clapping and drumming of women to a more varied instrumentation including the use of electronic instruments and male voices. One major change in chutney performance practice has been its incorporation into carnival space which has invited renewed and vigorous contemplation on issues of ethnicity.

Miller (1994) outlines the kinds of stereotypes that are used to reinforce ideas of difference in Trindad and notes how these discourses overshadow ethnicities other than "Indian" or "African". For him, the locations for ascribing difference have shifted. Post–World War II sees Indian communities still representing a peasantry with memories of indentureship, high levels of illiteracy, and Hindu marriage only just gaining legal recognition. For Africans, by contrast, slavery is already distant and they move about in the "modern world". The early 1980s and the oil boom still see Africans generally earning higher incomes than Indians, but by the late 1980s, Indian communities are witnessing rapid change with entry into banking and media jobs, migration, for instance to Canada, and greater political prominence.

Miller notes an absence of discussion on processes of "Indianization" corresponding to these changes, while evidence for "creolization" is by contrast more widely acknowledged. He turns to an example of an Indian woman, Drupatee, singing in the 1988 and 1989 carnival seasons to highlight the increasing participation of Indians at carnival as an aspect of creolization. His interpretation of Drupatee's carnival presence is interesting with regard to developments in chutney performance during the 1990s. What was a successful "Indian version of soca" and hence evidence for creolization, seemed to Miller to be "taking over from an older tradition of syncretic chutney music [sic]" (1994, 280). Drupatee's late 1980s repertoire could be seen, in fact, as exploring the boundaries between chutney and soca. Miller's interpretation reduces Drupatee's performances to being merely reflective of ethnic divisions and conforming to, what were at that time, dominant narratives about which musics were "national". In taking a retrospective view, however, one can suggest an alternative interpretation, which is that such performances are an integral aspect of socioeconomic and political changes within, as well as between, various ethnic communities in Trinidad.[2] Rather than simply affirming creolization processes, Drupatee's involvement with carnival marked the more general entry of Indian performers who took chutney repertoires into this performance context. While Indian musicians had long been a part of carnival, albeit in small numbers, neither female performers nor chutney music had hitherto established a niche in carnival.

In addition to questions about the origin and musical value of chutney, this is also a tradition which, for some people, represents the Indian response to (rather than the Indian version of) calypso. Furthermore, chutney has been used to establish a distinctive performance space in carnival. In interviews that appeared in the *Trinidad Guardian* in 1996, some schoolchildren were asked why they thought that chutney had been so popular during the carnival celebrations that year. Here are some of their comments:

Maurisa Ramsingh: "I think its popularity is due to the 'coalition' government because this represents the coming together of two races [African and Indian]. Chutney has now become a major force in uniting the two races."

Patel Grant: "It is popular because of the continued pattern in which Stalin [a calypsonian] won the Calypso Monarch competition last year with Sundar Popo [chutney singer]."

Simon Williams: "[I]t represents a coming together of two cultures."

Richard Payle: "I think that chutney has become popular because the calypsonians of East Indian descent have brought forward their culture, and because of this the other races have adopted what the Indian calypsonians have brought forward." (cited in the *Trinidad Guardian*, 17 February 1996, 9, no author)

These are commentaries on the political significance of chutney, on the interaction between calypso and chutney – and on a more general level between "two cultures". The commentaries reflect views on issues of ethnicity and the role played by music in society. In contrast to speculations about the Indianness or creolization of chutney, these schoolchildren do not posit a simple opposition between chutney and calypso.

Instead, they stress the kinds of musical interactions that are central in negotiating national culture. Their views are reiterated in other sources. The rhythm of "chutney soca", as a practice which draws on musical traditions from both India and Africa, has been described, for example, as "totally indigenous" (Baptiste 1993, 39).

Further parallels can be drawn between chutney and calypso on the basis of song competitions. Additional parallels include: the celebratory aspects of the music with an emphasis on dancing and on parties; a focus on the singer; and the range of topics addressed by the texts of the songs. Moreover, there is evidence of increasing interaction between chutney and calypso musicians with the participation of chutney artists in carnival and in the calypso tents, and with the entry of African-Caribbean musicians to chutney competitions. The second annual National Chutney Monarch competition (1996), modelled on calypso competitions, was approved by chutney and calypso organizations and the government: the National Association of Chutney Artists of Trinidad and Tobago, the Trinbago Unified Calypsonians Organization, the Ministry of Community Development, Culture, and Women's Affairs, and the Carnival/Cultural Judges Association of Trinidad and Tobago. Chutney and calypso, therefore, are not performance events exclusive to a specific ethnic group. The use of the term "chutney soca" is evidence of the influence of calypso and it is sometimes used to describe the genre (as it has been presented in the public arena).

While there is certainly evidence of musical exchange and chutney performers adopting calypso models of transmission and competition, chutney is becoming increasingly significant at the level of cultural policy-making in Trinidad. It is seen as a performance forum giving a voice to Indians in the Caribbean and as contributing to a World Music market. The global and local spaces of the World Music market and carnival in Trinidad are intimately related. As in the case of zouk in the French-speaking Antilles, for example, representations of national culture in the international market help to reformulate local self-images (Guilbault 1993). These reformulations raise questions at government level concerning the promotion and support of musical performances.

These were points evident in a speech given by the minister of community development, culture and women's affairs, Daphne Phillips, at a symposium (the first of its kind) titled "Carnival, Calypso and Chutney in Contemporary Trinidad and Tobago Society" (April 1998). Phillips began with a statement "recognizing the nature and complexity of contemporary Trinidad and Tobago in all its dimensions" but suggested placing this complex society "in the context of the wider international milieu in which we exist, both in terms of the nature of market relations . . . as well as the growing consciousness of the political issue of democracy and freedom of expression on the one hand, and human rights principles on the other". Her assessment of chutney and calypso is unequivocal: "in their historical emergence and contemporary contexts, [they] are of profound cultural and political significance to the Trinidad and Tobago society in general, and to ethnic groups in particular". But even if chutney and calypso are seen as being important to particular ethnic groups, Phillips concludes that "culture and our creative art forms have now become a dynamic forum for equity and national unity" (Phillips 1998, 10–11). Her assessment is illuminating. While indicating the importance of specific musics to different ethnic groups because of the ways in which they remind people of the distinct historical experiences of the nation's citizens, she concludes on an optimistic note. These musics offer a medium for shaping and expressing national unity. It is an aspiration that takes diversity into account.

Most of Phillips's speech focuses on policies implemented with regard to the support of carnival which include: a decentralization of carnival managerial responsibilities in response to requests from artists for greater control of their own carnival space; the establishment of a carnival institute for preservation, documentation, research and development work and the provision of undergraduate scholarships, funding for lectureships, library materials and resources for the new Bachelor of Science in Pan degree at the University of the West Indies. These policies indicate the extent to which Phillips has institutionalized the concept of carnival and reinforced it as the representation of national identity in public speech and thereafter in the mainstream press. Indeed Phillips noted that "the state is aware of the role of culture in national development and . . . it is willing to use its power and resources to influence efficiency, research, training, business development, people participation, self-sufficiency, artistic integrity, equity and fairness" (1998, 11). The rhetoric of cultural policy-making confirms van Koningsbruggen's view that it is in carnival "the annual event par excellence in which artistic skills and imagination are combined for a single large-scale creative and reflective display of social and cultural values – that the society recognizes itself and wishes to take itself seriously" (1997, 168). The symposium theme was an important step towards a realization of the repeated emphasis on equity because it brought together three major strands of Trinidad and Tobago's cultural life for consideration and debate. Since chutney is now being heralded as the Indian contribution to carnival, it provides another medium for exploring ideas about national culture.

## ISSUES OF IDENTITY IN CHUTNEY SONG TEXTS

Many chutney song texts are repetitive. The structure is usually alternating verse and chorus. I have selected some examples which highlight the ways in which chutney texts create a sense of relatedness, of belonging, first by exploring the experiences and everyday concerns of Indian-Caribbean people, and second, by the naming of specific places – in the Caribbean or elsewhere – with large Indian-Caribbean populations. The named places in the following examples include Guyana, Trinidad (specifically the Trinidadian villages of Penal and Sangre Grande), the United States and Canada.

Some of the song texts used centre around themes of marriage and courtship. These are the themes with which women, in private contexts, must have been concerned on such occasions as preparing a bride for a wedding. A thread of continuity is thus provided, with the transition of chutney from private to public spheres, through its narrative content. The song texts are those of some of the most successful chutney singers. These include Sundar Popo, Anand Yankaran, Drupatee Ramgoonai, all from Trinidad, and Terry Gajraj (from the village Fyrish, in Guyana).

### Example 3.1: Sundar Popo (text transcribed from JMC cassette JMC-1113, 1995)[3]

"Indian Arrival"

The Fatel Rozack came from India
with me *nanee* [maternal grandmother] and me *nana* [maternal grandfather]
and some landed here.
They brought with them their language, Urdu and Hindi,
their culture: Hosein, Phagwa, Ramlila and Divali.

. . . Like brother and sister

in the boat they came, singing and playing their *tabla*.
Remember 1845, the thirteenth of May
Two hundred and twenty-five immigrants who landed on that day.

Early every morning, the bells ring louder
to labour agriculture so their children wouldn't suffer,
sugar cane, cocoa, coconut, rice and banana.

Together with me *agee* [paternal grandmother] and me *agaa*
[paternal grandfather],
labour was cheap but food was cheaper
watch *penga* [money] come for flour
and *penga* come for rice
cent and a half for sugar
and everything was nice.

This song was released in the year when Indians were celebrating 150 years in Trinidad. Sundar Popo provided a well-known account of Indian migration to Trinidad and the labourers' experiences on the plantations, referring to the Fatel Rozack (or *Fath Al Razak*), sugar cane and other agricultural pursuits. This was one of the chutney songs composed in celebration of "Arrival Day".

### Example 3.2: Anand Yankaran (text transcribed from JMC cassette JMC-1112, 1996)

"Guyana Kay Dulahin"

*Guyana kay dulahin*
come to Trinidad
I want to be your *dulaha*.

(Bride from Guyana
come to Trinidad
I want to be your bridegroom.)

In this song text the bridegroom appeals for a bride not from India but from another Indian-Caribbean context. Through marriage, kinship ties are thereby strengthened between Indian-Caribbean nationals from Trinidad and Guyana, at the same time as they are weakened between the

Caribbean and the ancestral homeland, India. On the other hand, the continued use of kinship terms such as *dulaha* and *dulahin* is one of the clearest examples of preservation of language.

**Example 3.3: Terry Gajraj (text transcribed from a cassette recording, 1994)**

"Guyana Baboo"

Me come from de country they call Guyana
land of de bauxite, de rice and sugar . . .
Singing in the US and Canada
I am coming back man, back to Guyana . . .
I am coming back, back to Guyana
to find me a *dulahin* for this *dulaha*.

Whereas Indians began migrating to the Caribbean in 1838, a more recent Indian-Caribbean migration to the United States and to Canada began during the 1980s. Terry Gajraj is a chutney singer whose lyrics draw upon his experiences in Guyana. The description of Guyana as the land of rice and sugar reminds the listener of plantation agriculture, which has been so important for the island economy and which played a pivotal role in transporting Indian populations to the Caribbean. Having migrated to a diasporic context which is home to Indian-Caribbean communities (North America), the singer as the protagonist in this song nonetheless emphatically identifies himself with the Caribbean. This identification is done through repetition of the phrase, "I am coming back." He intends to find a bride from the Caribbean, thereby strengthening his affiliation to Guyana (as in example 3.2) by kinship ties. Again, the kinship terms *dulahin* and *dulaha* are used.

Similar sentiments are expressed in other chutney texts. The use of other kinship terms (*nanee* [maternal grandmother]; *bhowji* [sister-in-law]), references to food (*baiganee* [an aubergine snack]; chutney; rice; *dhal* [split peas, similar to lentils]), and to instruments (*tassa* [drum]) are other representations of common experiences.

### Example 3.4: Drupatee Ramgoonai (1989)

Drupatee Ramgoonai describes musical interaction in the Caribbean and opposition to her own entry into the calypso world as follows:

"Indian Soca"

Indian soca, sounding sweeter,
hotter than a *chulha* [stove];
rhythm from Africa and India,
blend together is a perfect mixture.
All we do is add new flavour
Leh we get down to Indian soca.
They give me blows
Last year for doing soca
But it shows
How much they know about culture
For the music of the steeldrums from Lavantille
Cannot help but mix with rhythm from Caroni
For it's a symbol of how much we've come of age
Is a brand new stage.

### Example 3.5: Sundar Popo (text transcribed from JMC cassette JMC-1082, 1994)

"Phoulourie"

*Chorus*
*Phoulourie bina chutney* [phoulourie without chutney]
*Kaisay banee* [that's all that I'm preparing].

*Verses*
I went Sangre Grande
to meet Lal Beharry . . .
I beating my drum
and I singing my song
the only thing I missing
is my bottle of rum . . .
Me and my darling

was flying in a plane
the plane catch a fire
and we fell inside the cane . . .
Jack and Jill went up the hill
to fetch a pail of water
Jack fell down and broke his thumb
and Jill came tumbling after.
Little Jack Horner
Sat in a corner
eating his Christmas pie . . .

Many different themes are raised in this song. Sangre Grande, phoulourie without chutney, the drum, the bottle of rum, the cane – these are all images of local village life. The inclusion of the nursery rhymes in this chutney song is an example of those cultural elements which have been absorbed in the tradition as a result of historical circumstance and interaction between people from diverse places. But this is a brief appearance of any "British" elements; perhaps the use of the English language is the biggest British impact on the chutney tradition. This is certainly Manuel's view. He notes that Trinidad "remains host to a number of distinctly non-English music traditions" (Manuel 1995, 184).

## KINSHIP THEMES IN CHUTNEY SONG TEXTS

The preceding examples of chutney song texts indicate the kinds of themes raised which lead to audience reflection on issues of identity in general terms. Song texts also deal with kinship relations as a way of further exploring relatedness amongst Indian-Caribbean communities. Song texts that comment inappropriately on certain kinship relations have provoked heated debate and criticism for these are relations of vital importance (Klass 1961, chapter 4).

Through their song texts, chutney singers challenge notions of kinship and redefine accepted kinship and gender roles. Sonny Mann's "Loota La" (NSCD 015, track 5), was one of the most prominent examples. The award of the title Chutney Monarch (1995) indicates that the song was generally well received despite the ferocious criticism it also attracted. Several variants were released later, including a collaborative recorded performance with the soca singer Denise Belfon and the ragga singer General Grant (CR1296, Rituals Label, *Caribbean Party Rhythm 1*, track 46) and Sally Edwards' interpretation in which the instrumental accompaniment of Mann's version, *dholak*, *dhantal* and harmonium, is augmented with keyboards, drum machine, synthesized brass and bass (NSCD 032, track 3).

Klass writes that a joking relationship is permitted between the wife of a man and his younger brother but it is one with limits. "Joking consists of remarks on personal appearance ('Man, you ugly!'), dress, and habits, plus playful slapping, ear-pulling, etc. There are definite bounds, however, and speech or action which was overtly sexual would be frowned upon" (1961, 101–2). The *bhowji* that Sonny Mann sings about therefore behaves in an unacceptable fashion. The narrative was shocking to many because of the public performance contexts in which it was presented. The controversial reception to this song is paralleled in the north Indian context. The theme of an adulterous relationship between a married woman and her younger brother-in-law is a common one in north Indian folk and folk-pop songs. The dissemination of these songs in public performance arenas through the spread of cassette technology has led to concerns about appropriate performance contexts and increasing obscenity in the texts (see Manuel 1993, 172–76). In north India, the commercial marketing of such songs, which are mainly sung by male professionals, is orientated towards a male audience. Chutney in the Indian-Caribbean context does not demonstrate a similar kind of gender distinction. Men and women perform chutney and buy recordings.

The interpretation of many chutney song texts in a national forum relies on a knowledge of kinship relations among, and the social concerns of, Indian-Caribbean people. Apparently trivial lines provide images of everyday life, for example, "grind *masala*". They may also be statements which can be read in relation to attitudes concerning the public display of female dancing, for example, "wine *beti*" (*beti* being a daughter or the daughter of a sibling or cousin). "Roll up the *tassa*" is both an invitation to dance and a herald to the arrival of the principal participants in a wedding ceremony.

Henry's (1973) study of village music in north India is significant here, in relation to the tracing of chutney's origin to ritual contexts, and not just because it provides comparative material on wedding songs. (Henry examines song texts associated with the wedding ritual in the Bhojpuri speaking regions of Uttar Pradesh and Bihar.) It is his assessment of women's music performed at weddings that is relevant. He argues that it is the "innermost" music of the village for two reasons: it is sung in the home and it deals with kinship and family rituals. His study is further significant because in his discussion of "inner" and "outer" musics and in his search for related material he turns to Arya's (1968) study of songs from Suriname. Henry finds similarities between his material and that of Arya and even some identical song texts. Thus women's "innermost" music has migrated to the Indian diaspora and from there to an Indian-Caribbean diaspora (especially in Britain, Holland, the United States and Canada). In moving between "inner" and diasporic spheres, Henry's study is a reminder that the significance of kinship themes in chutney song texts extends beyond a local performance arena. Chutney singers play an important role in representing images of Indian-Caribbean communities to "others".

One of the most frequently explored themes in chutney song texts is that of the *dulahin* (daughter-in-law, bride). Depictions of the *dulahin* do not generally provoke criticism of the kind directed at songs about the *bhowji*. Klass notes that to her husband's family, the *dulahin* "is an object of considerable suspicion. Will she respect her new husband and his parents? Will she be obedient? Will she work hard? Can she learn to do things their way?" (1961, 114–15). Until the birth of a grandchild she is an "outsider". The male chutney singer often sings of wanting to find a *dulahin* (as in examples 3.2 and 3.3). In many song texts the male singer also encourages the *dulahin* to dance.

The image of the Indian-Caribbean woman in her role as *dulahin* has undergone radical change in recent chutney song texts. Once seen as the keeper of tradition she is now seen as an agent who is increasingly independent from her male counterpart, who flaunts her sexuality openly and consorts with whomever she likes. In doing so she is not necessarily portrayed as abandoning tradition but as bringing it with her into a public performance space. She still wears her sari if she wants to, she is still urged to "grind *masala*", and she is still compelled to dance on hearing the *dhantal* and *dholak*. Compare the following extracts from three song texts. The first is a love song by the calypsonian, Mighty Sparrow, sung to an Indian-Caribbean woman. The Indian-Caribbean woman to whom Sparrow sings conforms to all the traditional expectations of her community. The last line, "jump out of time to sweet pan for carnival" is noteworthy here in relation to the following examples, for it is an indirect suggestion that her participation in carnival would be an incompetent one. The song "Marajhin" is part of a trilogy (1982, transcribed from a 1992 recording by BLS Records, a company based in the Virgin Islands, BLS-1015).[4] I include this text here because the imagery that Sparrow draws on deals with the same kinds of Indian-Caribbean themes found in chutney songs (compare the following examples) and its presentation in national public performance spaces foreshadowed chutney's entry to the same performance arena. Warner notes that this song text resorts "to the now classic references to Indian foods, and their preparation, to the supposed strictness of the Indian parents, to Indians' purported penchant for violence, to their clothing, and even to their supposed inability to keep the same time as 'real' Trinidadians" (1993, 287). To this list can be added the reference to the *dulahin* (who is Marajhin in this case) in the chorus. In terms of musical texture, Sparrow also drew on "Indian-Caribbean" instrumental timbres by including *dhantal* and *dholak*. The comparison between chutney and calypso song texts highlights both as important public mediums for social commentary. The comparison also highlights both as mediums which provoke wider debates on issues of gender, ethnicity and identity in the national forum (see Constance 1991 and Warner 1993 for further discussion of these debates in relation to calypso).

### Example 3.6: Marajhin (text transcribed from BLS cassette BLS-1015, 1992)

I will tell you true the way I feel for you
I'll do anything to make you happy
So if you think it's best to change me style of dress
I will wear a *caphra* [cotton suit] or a *dhoti* [cloth wrapped around the waist]
I'll give you a modern *jupa* [wooden house] down in Penal
And I'll change my name to Rooplal or Sparrowlal
I could learn to grind *masala* [spice] and *chunka-dhal* [ground lentils]
And jump out of time to sweet pan for carnival.

Examples 3.7 and 3.8 are heard on a compact disc compilation aimed at a World Music market (NSCD 032).[5] The song texts comment on topics of local relevance but are presented to a global market. In this compilation contrasting images of the *dulahin* are found. By now, the *dulahin* has learnt how to "move to the rhythm and . . . to the beat". She is at home in "calypso city". She wears her mini skirt or her sari. This is a girl who can forget tradition, who is "plenty fun" and who can party at "soca paradise".

## Example 3.7: Double D's "Ragga Dulahin" (NSCD032, track 5)

*Verse*
She move to the rhythm and she move to the beat
It busy like allow how she looking sweet
She coming on the dance with a short short mini
She come with Double D and she leave with Ronnie.
She wearing high cut mini
She go with she sari
Wine like tiny winey
Don't care who really see.

*Chorus*
I have a ragga *dulahin* (x 4)
Come roll *beti*, roll *beti*, roll up the *tassa*
Grind *beti*, grind *beti*, grind up *masala*
Roll *beti*, roll *beti*, roll up the *tassa*
Me say grind *beti*, grind *beti*, grind up *masala*
I have a ragga *dulahin* (x 4)
Oooh, She raise she sari and she party
she raise she sari and she party
Oooh, She raise she sari and she party
She raise she sari and she party

*Verse*
Come let we jam with the demolition man . . .
All in the party, they come from away
Ah *dulahin* in calypso city
Guyana posse . . .
Ah *dulahin* inside in the party
Come jump around with the bunch in Trini.
. . . Forget the tradition

This girl is plenty fun
She come and wine down low
It's massive Trinbago
I have a ragga *dulahin* . . .

## Example 3.8: Madain Ramdas (NSCD032, track 9)

"Chutney Genie"

*Chorus*
Darling put on your high heels, your mini and your tights
Le we go and fete in soca paradise tonight
Soca paradise! Soca paradise.
Le we go and fete in soca paradise tonight.
Darling put on your high heels, your mini and your tights
I want you to be my chutney genie tonight.

*Verse*
When I look into your eyes girl I don't know what to do
Don't know what to do girl. I don't know what to do
All about my body I could feel your shadow
When the *dholak* and *dhantal* start to ring like a bell
Genie it's time now for you to cast your spell
Le we go and fete in New York city tonight.
New York city! New York city!
. . . Le we jam the chutney in Miami tonight
Le we jam the soca in Miami tonight.

In these song texts the Indian-Caribbean woman is depicted as having broken away from the ethnic enclaves which still restricted Sparrow's involvement with her. She "jams with the demolition man". She "comes with Double D and leaves with Ronnie". She is in fact partying all over the Indian-Caribbean diaspora (New York, Miami). Sparrow would no longer have to change his name to Sparrowlal or Rooplal.

Other song texts in the same compact disc compilation (examples 3.9 and 3.10) present a different view of expectations of the Indian-Caribbean woman. These texts reveal attempts to place restrictions on women by emphasizing their private duties rather than depicting their public roles, thereby circumscribing their domestic role in society. In example 3.9, the "doltish boy" is reproached for he carries out the duties of his wife which include minding the pot in the kitchen and working in the yard:

## Example 3.9: Sundar Popo

"Doltish Boy"

*Chorus*
You doltish or what, boy,
you doltish or what,
always in the kitchen, minding the pot
your wife in the house, polishing she nails
and you in the yard boy, working out your tail.

Chutney singers also play on the fears of some commentators that chutney leads to the break-up of the home. These texts present the kind of critique that is levelled at female chutney audience participants. While in example 3.9 the husband is chided, in example 3.10 the singer himself assumes the role of the disapproving husband. He is nevertheless unable to prevent his wife from joining in chutney and can only threaten to leave her. These texts present images of reversed gender roles:

## Example 3.10: Anand Yankaran

"Darling I Go Leave You"

*Verse*
I can't live your saga girl life, I prefer to live without a wife.
I does have to cook, wash and sweep up the house,
every time I talk you want to bust up me mouth . . .
I does have to wash and press your saga girl pants,
every time you have to go to a dance.
I does have to stay at home and mind your baby,
if I don't get mad I go get crazy.

*Chorus*
Darling I go leave you here alone, I packing my baggage and I going home.

The images of the *dulahin* in the examples above are diverse and contrasting and can be interpreted in different ways. The inward-looking approach of considering these texts in relation to kinship systems provides a framework for a hermeneutic reading of these chutney song texts. But there is no escaping the involvement of chutney in a wider public stage as musicians reach out to larger audiences. The song texts themselves point to a wider performance arena and to the movements of the *dulahin* beyond the island space of Trinidad. Music marketing terminology of "crossover" also points to wider performance arenas. Thus new crossover developments in chutney include chutney-bangra [bhangra], hip hop "soca bangra" and bangra-wine (Jean Michel Gibert, managing director, Rituals, personal communication, 1998). Such rhetoric is reproduced, too, in the information set out on the World Wide Web by Rituals (the Trinidad and Tobago company that licensed some tracks to MCI for the NSCD label). In these Web pages we find statements such as the following:

These hot and groovy vibes are coming straight from the youth of Trinidad – where the "races and cultures" mix to create a new and up-tempo world music beat. Call it Rapso, Ragga soca, Chutney soca, Ragga, Dancehall, Hipso, these rhythms crossover with the R&B and Hip Hop influences enhanced by a deep Calypso Soca Steelband musical background. This is the music of the world groove DJ's, the reflection of globalisation of our Planet Earth." (New Vibes, www.rituals.com)

## CHUTNEY IN LONDON

Other chutney spaces in the global ecumene provide the conditions for further musical exchanges – the crossovers of marketing rhetoric. These spaces also highlight why this genre must be considered in the context of an Indian-Caribbean (not just an Indian-Trinidadian) identity. Throughout the Indian-Caribbean diaspora, chutney shows have provided a means to celebrate ties to the Caribbean and to meet with other members of the diasporic community. The example I turn to and the interlinking of place discussed here (Trinidad and London) are related to interlinking histories and to the transmission of chutney through diasporic networks that look to the Caribbean as the homeland. Caryl Phillips observes that much British history is little known, "not least because much of it took place in India, Africa and the Caribbean" (quoted by Jaggi 1995). The historical forces which brought together Indian, British and Caribbean elements must be taken into account in tracing both the formation of an Indian-Caribbean identity and the development of the chutney tradition.

During the 1950s and 1960s, Caribbean nationals were recruited to fill the postwar labour shortage in the "mother country" (Britain). The descendants of Indian migrants to the Caribbean thus undertook a second migration, again in response to British policy. Although many of those who made the journey are Caribbean nationals of Indian descent, an Indian-Caribbean identity is still scarcely recognized in Britain. The experience of emigrating to a country which – despite ties on imperial, political and economic levels – did not feel like a homeland, brought issues of identity to the forefront. Questions of ethnicity and culture resurface in a new geographic context. Indian-Trinidadians in London were, until 1962 with the colony's independence from the empire, British citizens. They remained, however, visible "others" who maintained strong affiliations to the Caribbean, and who had a connection, from the more distant past, with India. The Race Equality Policy Group of the London Policy Unit was the first local authority department to recognize an Indian-Caribbean community, appointing an officer to liaise with community representatives in 1986. An Indo-Caribbean Cultural Association was set up in 1988. That the existence of the community is nevertheless little known is not surprising. For many Indian-Caribbean people a sense of belonging to a particular community is largely achieved through maintaining links with other Indian-Caribbean nationals, with friends, relatives, friends of friends and so on. Community events are infrequent. The occasional chutney perform-ances, with singers from the Caribbean, provide one of the few opportu-nities for a group expression of identity. The promotional posters for these events reveal some of the symbols of that identity. Some of these posters include illustrations of steel band, soca, parang and chutney. That such performances are organized at all is evidence of the links that are maintained between London's Indian-Caribbean community and the Caribbean.

Chutney shows began to be organized in London soon after chutney singers entered the arena of public performance in the Caribbean. Suresh Rambaran, who established G and H Promotions, played an important role in promoting chutney. As one of the first promoters of chutney music in London, he organized some performances as charity events to raise money to send to Trinidad. Before these public musical perform-ances, the main medium for exploring issues of identity was through literature and, indeed, a preoccupation with delineating identities is apparent in the writings of many Indian-Caribbean authors. In his opening address to the  conference on East Indians in the Caribbean (1979), Selvon commented:

I wrote a story once which was based on fact, about a Trinidad Indian who couldn't get a room to live in because the English landlord didn't want people from the Westindies, only bona fide Indians from the banks of the Ganges. So my boy posed as a true-true [real] Indian and got the room. But truth is even stranger than fiction, for when I applied to the Indian High Commission in London for a job, I was told that I was not an Indian because I came from Trinidad and was not born in India. (Selvon 1987, 17)

As a tradition that has developed in diasporic contexts, drawing upon diverse cultural and musical elements, chutney, too, is a reflection of the variety of identities adopted by individuals. This is true on a more general

Photo 6: Publicity poster for chutney show in London (produced by Saresh Rambaran, reproduced with permission).

Photo 7: Publicity poster for chutney show in London (produced by Saresh Rambaran, reproduced with permission).

level in considering Caribbean people in the diaspora and their musical choices. Manuel writes that "a typical New York West Indian may have various overlapping ethnic self-identities, for example, as Trinidadian, as West Indian, as Black, and . . . as American. Musical tastes reflect these intersections, as young West Indians grow up enjoying rap and R&B as well as the Sparrow in their parents' record collections" (Manuel 1995, 209–10).

Diversity in musical choices and overlapping identities are general features of what Slobin (1993) terms the "intercultural network" in his survey of the ways in which music travels to different parts of the world. How are these choices made? How are overlapping identities shaped? Taking into account the musical biographies of individuals is one way of probing the workings of an intercultural network. As an example, consider the musical biography of the Guyanese singer Terry Gajraj, who migrated to the United States during the 1980s. With his recording, Guyana Baboo (1994), Gajraj became one of the best selling recorded Indian-Caribbean singers. Traditional "Indian" elements have been transmitted to him through the family from one generation to another. His father taught him to play the accordion, the harmonica and the guitar. He learnt some Hindi and singing from his grandfather, who was a *pundit* (Hindu priest). By the age of six, Gajraj was performing at his family's *mandir* (temple). The music of ritual and the traditions transmitted through the family have been combined with other musical influences. He later freelanced with soca groups (the Original Pioneers and Melody Makers) and performed at weddings, fairs and estate dances. In 1989, like many other young Caribbean nationals seeking their fortunes, he moved to the United States, where his recording career was launched due to a fortunate set of circumstances and chance meetings. During the 1990s, he was invited to perform in the calypso tents at the Trinidad carnival. His own evaluation of his chutney style is that he blends Indian songs with influences from soca, reggae and rap. From his base in New York he travels to different performance venues, including different cities in the United States and in Canada, the Caribbean (as a chutney singer and as a calypsonian) and London. The diverse influences which we find in the musical biography of this singer are those that constitute the tradition of chutney too.

A performance given by Terry Gajraj in London in 1995 attracted approximately four hundred people – a good turnout, according to the organizers. The venue was a school hall which had been hired for the evening. Beer from the Caribbean and Indian food like *roti* (bread) and chicken curry was sold. Chutney in London, unlike in the Caribbean or amongst the Caribbean community in New York, is a little-known music that barely attracts audiences beyond the Indian-Caribbean community.

*Photo 8: A chutney audience in London at a performance given by Rikki Jai (photograph by Saresh Rambaran, reproduced with permission).*

The best-known Asian musical genre in Britain is *bhangra*, the music of "British Asian youth culture" (Baumann 1990), which emerged during the 1970s. Through bhangra, a reinvented Punjabi folk tradition which developed in London and in the Midlands, the Punjabi sphere of influence extends to other South Asian communities in Britain, the United States and Australia. Whether audiences are small or large, both chutney and bhangra are examples of popular musical genres which have developed in the diaspora, which cross many geographic, political and cultural boundaries and which are performed in urban centres like London. Both forms reveal influences from diverse sources. Bhangra musicians in London and in the Midlands, like chutney musicians in Trinidad, have looked to African-Caribbean models of musical expression. Yet bhangra as a reinvented and recontextualized tradition is rooted in a folk tradition from a defined region – the Punjab. By contrast, the origins of chutney beyond the Caribbean are difficult to trace. Bhojpuri traditions may be dominant among the Indian-Caribbean population, but elements incorporated from different regions in India together with those from local contexts in the Caribbean also contribute to chutney.

## MULTILOCAL BELONGING

Exchanges between travellers, and experiences in the New World, led to the development of new traditions and identities as soon as the first indentured labourers from India undertook the journey over the *kala pani* (black water) to Trinidad. Recent changes in the tradition – the move from private to public performance, the entry of chutney into carnival and the increasing links between chutney and other Caribbean musical genres – all have political importance. The arrival of chutney at the forefront of popular culture has coincided with an Indian-Caribbean ascent to political power, which culminated with the election of an Indian-Caribbean prime minister, Basdeo Panday, in Trinidad and Tobago. In Guyana, an Indian-Caribbean prime minister, Cheddi Jagan, had been elected as early as 1953, as leader of the People's Progressive Party. Chutney shows create a sense of relatedness between Indian-Caribbean people via the use of what are perceived to be Indian elements from the ancestral homeland. These elements are a cultural heritage on the one hand, and the result of a continuing interaction with India on the other.

Yet chutney is an Indian-Caribbean tradition and performances are ways of negotiating spaces in national frameworks. Chutney singers incorporate the musical procedures of other, better-known Caribbean traditions, and aim to reach as wide an audience as possible. An Indian-Caribbean identity is affirmed amidst the contrasting claims made about the tradition. Whether the tradition is described as an authentic Indian one, or whether it is perceived as the result of musical interaction in the Caribbean, debates regarding chutney occur in the context of asserting an Indian identity in the Caribbean, not in India. The debate is about protecting Indian culture in the Caribbean from other powerful influences on one hand, and about celebrating the Indian contribution to the diverse cultural life of the Caribbean on the other. The political significance of chutney partly accounts for the vast differences in the reception of the tradition in Trinidad and in London. In Trinidad, chutney is now another established popular genre which is taken as a general representation and articulation of an ethnic group within the national space. In London, it is hardly known outside the relatively small Indian-Caribbean community. Performances are advertised to, and attended by, members of the Indian-Caribbean community.

Performance spaces in both Trinidad and London and the multiplicity of ties to different places, however, highlight chutney as giving expression to a sense of multilocal belonging. While chutney contributes to diaspora discourse, it does so by providing people with a sense of the place of home, in the instances discussed here, in Trinidad or in London. Avtar Brah argues that "the concept of diaspora embodies a subtext of 'home'" (1996, 190). This concept places "the discourse of 'home' and 'dispersion' in creative tension, inscribing a homing desire while simultaneously critiquing discourses of fixed origins". Brah observes that while the idea of a homeland elsewhere is integral to the diasporic condition "not all diasporas inscribe homing desire through a wish to return to a place of 'origin'" (1996, 192–93). This is certainly pertinent in relation to Indian-Caribbean communities in Trinidad and London. By looking at the status of chutney as an Indian-Caribbean form, I have been trying to show how performances of this music give people (wherever "home" is) a sense of belonging to many places – to India, to the Caribbean, to particular villages in Trinidad and to Britain. Musical exchanges contribute to the sense of multilocal belonging.

# From Wedding Ritual to Popular Culture

The study of the history of a musical culture as well as observation of musical practice during the course of field research undoubtedly reveals new perspectives on musical changes. Yet historical accounts may tell us more about the "myths" through which a musical culture "contemplates and presents itself", to borrow a phrase from Treitler (1993, 23), than about music from the past and its relation to present forms. While representations of chutney's past are not uniform and depend on the perspective of the teller, it is mainly with one kind of historical representation that this chapter is concerned: the perceived transformation of *mathkor* into the popular genre, chutney. Considering assertions of a particular musical genealogy – *mathkor* to chutney – is a way of exploring the social and cultural significance of chutney in Trinidad, particularly in relation to intergender and interethnic interaction.

The singer, Rawatie Ali, emphatically located the origins of chutney in Hindu wedding rituals, specifically in the *mathkor* ceremony. "Don't let anybody tell you otherwise!" she exhorted.[1] Such a location is enjoying much currency (see Baksh-Soodeen 1991; Ribeiro 1992; Kanhai 1995), but it is not the sole origin theory. If we therefore accept the diverse sources which have contributed to the construction of chutney as a popular genre, this historical representation could be regarded as being as much an interpretative move as it is based on knowledge of chutney's history. Yet its emergence as a focal point in historical representations can be explained in relation to women's celebration of the extension of the family through new kinship ties (formed by marriage or birth) in rites like *mathkor*. Thus the memory of chutney as a popular genre which emerges from hitherto female traditions performed at specific rituals is important in maintaining a sense of relatedness and it is therefore important as a marker of an Indian-Caribbean identity. But chutney, as we shall see, is not accepted by everyone as being either a fitting representation of Indian-Caribbeanness or even as suitable for public performance.

## MATHKOR AS WOMEN'S TRADITION

The performance of *mathkor* can be analysed in terms of the preservation and continuity of traditions from the Indian ancestral land. It continued to be performed in Trinidad as part of the Sanatanist Hindu wedding ritual. Sanatanists, as followers of *Sanatan Dharm* (literally "eternal duty or religion"), observe a generalized form of Hinduism found amongst many diasporic Indian communities (see Vertovec 1992).

There is an entry in George Grierson's *Discursive Catalogue of Bihar Peasant Life* (1885) on *mathkor* in the Indian context. Grierson called it *mathkorwa* (as do women in Trinidad who are now in their seventies and eighties).[2] The catalogue is a valuable source of historical and ethnographic data, giving us some insights into ceremonies, practices and objects found in Bihar over a century ago. Grierson described *mathkor* as an important ritual forming part of a Hindu wedding in the following terms:

The women of the family, and their friends, go singing to a well. They level a piece of ground near the well and smooth it down with *lal mati*, a kind of yellow clay which is generally found immediately over gravel. They then dig a clod up out of it, and carry it home on the head of one of them. They make a fireplace, *chulha*, of this mud in the centre of the courtyard or *angan*. In South Bhagalpur they set up a plantain tree and a bamboo in the courtyard, under which they place the mud. (1885, 362)

In Trinidad, one of the earliest written references to *mathkor* is found in Harry Ramnath's book, *India Came West*, dating from the 1960s. Ramnath describes and explains the symbolic and spiritual significance of *mathkor* as follows:

*Mathkor* literally means dirt digging . . . This *pujan* [religious ceremony] is the honouring of Mother Earth from whence all physical things have their beginnings. On the afternoon just before the *pundit* [priest] performs the first ceremony to commence the wedding . . . the mother [both of the bride and of the groom] along with close relatives and friends go to a place where the intended ceremony will be performed. The spot must be free from refuse or waste matter, preferably near a river, lake or pond . . . On this spot the mother takes clean water brought with her or water from the river or pond so long as the water is clean. She must use her right hand and sprinkle the water on the spot . . . After washing her hands she takes water again from a bronze goblet or *lota* and sprinkles the spot again. This time the significance is that the spot is being made pure or cleansed.

. . . The mother will thank Mother Earth who had blessed and afforded her this great opportunity to have a child who is to be married . . . During the time when the mother is performing her rituals, lady relatives and friends beat drums, and dance to appropriate songs to Mother Earth and other deities. (Ramnath n.d., 97–98)

In villages in south Trinidad I asked women about the *mathkor* ceremony:

I remember my sister's wedding. I was only a child at the time. My aunt gave me a lot of money because it would have been my turn next to get married. The day before the wedding all the women came to our house and we all went down to the river. We always went to the river Orupouche [sic]. They were singing, dancing and playing drums. They put saffron on my sister's forehead and painted her hands . . ."

I saw when the neighbour opposite was going to get married. All the women dressed in their saris started singing and dancing outside the house. They were going to the river. Some of them were playing the drums. I could have gone but I was in the shop. (Accounts of women from a village in south Trinidad, collected July 1996)

*Mathkor*, as women's pre-wedding celebration, with the ritual bathing, the drumming, singing and dancing, can be traced to cultural practices in India. The *dholak*, for example, is still played as a domestic instrument in the north of India. The use of the drum by women in Trinidad seems to be a continuation of a tradition "depicted in Mughal and provincial court sources, where it was played by the women of the palace to accompany birth and wedding songs and sometimes also dance" (Dick 1984, 562). The importance of going to the riverside in the accounts above is parallelled by the widespread practice in India of pre-wedding ritual bathing, the *ban*. There are similarities between the pre-wedding celebrations in India and in Trinidad, but the important points here are first, that wedding songs constitute "a major part of India's folksong tradition" (Wade 1980, 150), and second, that they are sung by women. The songs are "rich in documentation about family lineage" (Wade 1980, 150). Whatever the social restrictions, then, Indian-Caribbean women who continued these performances played a vital role in celebrations marking the expansion of the family and were the carriers of musical traditions; folksong in particular.

In Grierson's and Ramnath's accounts, women perform the ceremony and provide music and dance. In fact, *mathkor* is regarded as being a ceremony in which only women should participate. The drumming, singing and dancing which follow the religious rite, used to take place inside the house. Only women and children (including boys) were allowed to participate or observe (James Ramsawak, personal interview July 1996). The restrictions placed on who would be able to take part in the ceremony stemmed from the overtly sexual content of the song texts and dance. Vertovec, in his reference to *mathkor*, describes the dances as "highly suggestive" (1992, 203). It was considered demeaning for a man to sing these songs and he would be taunted for singing a woman's song (Ramaya 1990, 5). This attitude has now been overturned but it prevailed when chutney first began to emerge as male performance because of this genre's association with the wedding context.

However, male musicians have been involved with wedding music, usually providing instrumental backing. In a recent guide to the proper performance of the *mathkor* ceremony the presence of male musicians is implied:

The ladies accompanied by the drummers will go to a place where water can be available and preferably in the direction where the bride or groom lives. If there is not any water, then some of the water carried can be brought back. Some earth (dirt) has to be brought back as well. When they have reached the place, the Mati Kor [*mathkor*] (digging of the dirt) takes place. This ritual is for the appeasement of the elements: earth, air, fire, water and ether, to favour the bride/groom . . . After this the ladies return with the accompaniment of dancing to the tune of the drum beating. (Persad 1988, 7)

Photo 9: Tassa *drummers at a wedding ceremony in Trinidad*

In villages in the south of Trinidad, a *tassa* group is often employed to "beat drums" at wedding ceremonies. The *tassa* players are men (see photo 9). Moreover, the music and dance is no longer hidden. Even non-members of the wedding party, such as passers-by, can observe the ceremony and celebration which now takes place outdoors, in the open. Male musicians did in fact participate in these ceremonies during the 1960s at the time Ramnath wrote his account. One musician from a village in south Trinidad described his participation as a drummer in this kind of ritual: "When the ladies go upstairs on a Friday night they don't want any man going there . . . But as I am a drummer I get to go. I see everything, but what I do, I just bend down my head – I'm not seeing anything" (Baloon, personal interview, 1996).[3]

Apart from *tassa*, the instrumental timbres usually associated with *mathkor* (and with chutney) are *dholak* and *dhantal*. Nowadays, *tassa* groups together with recordings (of Indian film songs in particular) increasingly replace women vocalists accompanied by the *dhantal* and *dholak*, as music for dancing. Indeed, in Vertovec's description of "*muti kurwa*" only *tassa* drums are mentioned. Moreover, Vertovec states that during the intricate three-day set of wedding rites it is "old women" who "sing bawdy songs in Hindi" (1992, 203), suggesting that younger generations no longer learn these song traditions. Given the content of *mathkor* song texts, young women would be unlikely to sing them, but their performance is not confined to older women. Nevertheless, the performance styles of the *mathkor* ceremony have changed, within the ritual context as well as in its transformation in becoming part of popular culture. Yet women continue to dominate *mathkor* and, even though men may attend, it is perceived as being "more a woman's thing", as one man commented.

Although men's participation in the ceremony is more restricted, an intriguing historical account was narrated by Balkaransingh in which certain "categories" of men played an important role in the past. This account outlines a view of chutney's origins in those wedding and birth ceremonies in general to which men did not have ready access (including *mathkor*). The account makes a claim about a male role at such occasions being taken over by women in the diasporic context:

There's a group of people in India – they are an accepted part of society – called *hijras*. They are basically eunuchs. They go around from place to place at the births of babies and when people have been married. You see, in India there was a time when brides would be married very early. They wouldn't know much about what to expect. So these eunuchs . . . would be dressed in female clothes and they would go to the home of the bride, and in dance and music make those suggestive expressions to show the young person what to expect . . . When the Indians came to Trinidad they didn't bring eunuchs with them because they came as workers. But to carry on the tradition the women took that same role when young brides were being married. (Satnarine Balkaransingh, personal interview, 1996)[4]

Balkaransingh's description seems to apply to a separate, coexisting tradition rather than the private female performance contexts of *mathkor*. This is evident from the prominent role of women in India in wedding folksong traditions and the continued tradition of men dressing as women in Trinidad and performing at wedding celebrations. His account, nevertheless, draws attention to an important aspect of such ceremonies. Whereas Ramnath and Persad highlight the symbolic and spiritual significance of *mathkor* (thanking Mother Earth, appeasing the elements), Balkaransingh introduces a functional aspect: imparting some sexual knowledge prior to the final marriage ceremony. His location of chutney's origins in the activities of the *hijras* also offers a different kind of historical representation. By linking chutney with *hijras* he makes a claim about its origins in male, as well as female, spheres of ritual and musical activity. As with the more specific *mathkor* origin view, it emphasizes the Indian origins of chutney. As such, a continuous thread of male participation in this kind of music and dance is drawn from ancestral India through the continuation of private performance in Trinidad to the recent emergence of male chutney performers (particularly singers) on public stages.

## Audience Reception

Myers reports from her fieldwork undertaken during the 1970s that there are two important types of wedding song, the *byah ke git* and *lachari*. She suggests that a villager (from Felicity) when referring to wedding songs is probably thinking of the "more serious *byah ke git*, unaccompanied responsorial strophic songs with long texts that comment on various stages in the wedding ceremony" (1984, 230). The *lachari*, however, are linked with chutney. Myers writes:

lachari are fast lively songs with instrumental accompaniment; the villagers often describe them as "hot" or "chutney". The terms are similar but not synonymous. Both hot songs and chutney songs can have risqué texts, but the villagers do not think that these "suggestive" poems are as "bad" as the "rude" calypso texts. (1984, 231)

The comparison that is introduced between *lachari* and calypso song texts in this description is relevant to the reception of chutney during the 1980s and 1990s. Chutney is often compared with calypso and both now occupy a national and public performance space. But chutney's authenticity as an Indian-Caribbean popular music partly rests on its emergence from a "ritual" context. While *mathkor* and chutney are perceived as related, the reception to each of these genres is markedly different. Contemporary chutney is judged as being as "bad" and "rude" as calypso. The influence of religious musical forms: wedding ritual music and sacred music like *bhajans*, identified in contemporary Indian-Caribbean chutney has been much criticized (in press articles, letters to the press, public forums and private discussions). Chutney introduces "music for God" into the secular arena.

While women legitimately dominate in the performance of *mathkor*, their participation in chutney has been a subject of contestation. This is in spite of the relation between the two genres and their stylistic similarities, particularly with regard to instrumental timbre (voice, *dhantal* and *dholak*) and dance style. *Mathkor* is a socially sanctioned religious ritual in which music and dance play an integral part. Features intrinsic to *mathkor*, namely a sexually explicit dance style in response to the instrumental timbres of *dhantal* and *dholak*, nevertheless, prompt heated objections in the context of chutney. "Today you find a lot of men going to hear the chutney shows. The dancing is a bit, you know, 'vulgar'. The women shake up the waist and I think that is why a lot of men go – to see the dance," one woman explained to me. Another woman told me, "I am so ashamed to think that Hindu women can get up and dance so when they hear chutney." The reasons why such objections are made to features that are regarded as essential in the context of the *mathkor* ritual, are interrogated in the ensuing discussion. Such an interrogation raises issues of intergender and interethnic interactions in Trinidad, which can be analysed as relations arising from a specific historical context. What follows is a consideration of intergender interaction amongst the Indian indentured labourers who migrated to Trinidad during the mid-nineteenth century.

## INDIAN MIGRATION TO TRINIDAD: INDENTURESHIP AND GENDER DISPARITY

Grierson's (1885) catalogue was published in Calcutta. Forty years before the publication of Grierson's work 231 passengers who came from southern and northern Bihar, Uttar Pradesh and Bengal, sailed from the Calcutta Harbour for Trinidad, as indentured labourers on the ship, the *Fath Al Razak*. The ship arrived at Port of Spain, Trinidad's capital, in May 1845. One hundred and ninety-eight men and 29 women disembarked (Samaroo 1995). These numbers are indicative of the sex-ratio disparity that prevailed during the period of indentureship. The scarcity of Indian women in the British Caribbean was to have a profound impact on the indentured immigrant Indian community and on the status and role of women in Indian-Caribbean society.

During the early stages of indentureship, Indian men were reluctant to form relationships with non-Indian women for fear of risking social disapproval. Having travelled to the Caribbean on five-year contracts with the possibility of returning to India, many of the labourers

regarded themselves as exiles and were not disinclined to claim a return passage, hoping to be readmitted into caste by performing certain expiatory rites.

Marrying a woman of a different race, or for that matter a low caste Indian woman, and taking her to his village was unthinkable as it would most likely involve the severing of family ties and connections and certainly caste expulsion. (Mangru 1987, 217)

The continuing Indian presence in the Caribbean with labourers from different castes working together and the shortage of women would eventually contribute to the breakdown of the caste system and to the practice of polyandry. This was not only because of the disparity between the numbers of female and male migrants, but also because the Hindu wedding ceremony was unrecognized by the colonial authorities. Quite simply, a man and woman who married following the procedures of a Hindu wedding ritual were not legally recognized as being husband and wife. Such rituals were described as "bamboo" weddings or, using a more derogatory term, as "Coolie" weddings. A bride who was married according to Hindu rites legally remained an unmarried woman and could be "re-sold" (attracting a bridal dowry) and remarried later for a higher price. Jealousies between men over the women with whom they sought alliances led, at its most horrific manifestations, to incidences of the murder of wives. The case of a young woman in British Guiana, Goirapa, which was brought up during discussions of the Indian marriage amendment bill in 1886, is illustrative. Goirapa "was married 'Coolie fashion' [following Hindu wedding rites] to Yadakana who later suspected that her parents intended to remove her from the matrimonial home and sell her to a prospective buyer. Realising that he had no legal claim over his wife, Yadakana murdered her to prevent such a sale" (Mangru 1987, 226).

The experiences of Indian women in the Caribbean certainly included those of subordination and restrictions "within the reconstituted Indian family structure" as well as oppression under the indentureship system, and subjection to "the sexual depredations of the white overseer class" (Poynting 1987, 231–32). Yet, as labourers and wage earners in the Caribbean, Indian women also managed to attain a degree of independence which they had not enjoyed before. In addition to social problems resulting in part from disproportionate numbers of men and women, conditions on the sugar plantations, around which the labourers' lives revolved, were harsh (Haraksingh 1987; Samaroo 1987), and their living conditions were uncomfortable. The labourers were accommodated in barracks which, at the outset, had been built only for Indians who went to Trinidad unaccompanied by women.[5] Of note here is the expected social and sexual restrictions placed on women, together with intergender conflict caused by women's increasingly independent economic status, which characterize the period of indentureship. These factors are also central to current debates concerning the appropriateness of chutney as public performance.

Initially regarding themselves as transient settlers, the majority of Indians chose to remain in Trinidad when indentureship was abolished in 1917. Conscious effort was put into retaining some traditional and religious practices from India. Women played an important role in the continued performance of folksong as part of ritual ceremonies. Just as women in India sing wedding songs that are central to folksong traditions, Indian women in the Caribbean are seen as the preservers of tradition with regard to the music and dance of wedding rituals in particular. A common view is that it is due to women maintaining these Indian traditions that enabled a popular genre like chutney to develop. Ann Marie Chadee, secretary to the National Association of Chutney Artistes, for example, wrote in the newspaper, the *Sunday Express*:

The Indian male no longer conducted any form of musical or cultural activities in dialectical [sic] Bhojpuri. The Indian female stood up to champion the cause. The exclusive enclaves of the Indian female *matiko* [*mathkor*], *barahi* and *chati* [ceremonies held twelve and six days after the birth of a child] in particular provided the secret womb for this long gestation that will give birth to the popular chutney. (Chadee 1995, 21)

Chadee uses an interesting metaphor. Despite gender disparity during the early period of indentureship, women as guardians of tradition provided a "secret womb". But chutney as the offspring of female ritual contexts takes us into very different performance spaces where Indian-Caribbean men as well as women forge and promote a new musical expression embodying current experiences.

## FROM *MATHKOR* TO CHUTNEY: CHANGES IN PERFORMANCE SPACES

According to Balkaransingh, the dance style of chutney is not "Indian" insofar as it incorporates "the pelvic gyrations of African mating dances" (personal interview 1996) which in Trinidad is better known as "wining".

Although Baksh-Soodeen agrees with Balkaransingh that "the sexual education of the Hindu girl begins at these [*mathkor*] dances", her testimony differs in several important respects. Baksh-Soodeen regards *mathkor* as a ceremony "practised exclusively by women" which was "probably fought for centuries ago by Indian women to express their sexuality collectively within Hinduism" and which was brought to Trinidad by women from "rural lower caste Indian communities". The dancing is "certainly not 'wining'" but is "distinctively Indian". Chutney dancing originates from dances performed at *mathkor*, but Hindu women have taken them "out of these cloistered ceremonies into the public arena of chutney festivals and competitions" (Baksh-Soodeen 1991, 7).

Performance context is one of the main differences between *mathkor* and chutney. The differences lie in the categorizations of female/male performance and private/public domains. *Mathkor* was a private, re-ligious and unrecorded ceremony in which female performers dominated. As such, the performance of the *mathkor* ceremony seems to accord with the model in which women's musical activity belongs to the realm of the private, in contrast to that of men which belongs to the public domain. But women's involvement in the public performance of chutney (as in other contemporary contexts, for example see Post 1994) contributes to a blurring of the private/public boundary. Chutney is a commercially recorded, public and popular genre which features male and female performers. The music performed at the *mathkor* ceremony is not known as "*mathkor* music" but simply as "local" music (Terry Gajraj, personal interview, 1996).[6] Chutney too could be described as "local" music for it developed in the Indian-Caribbean context. In response to my persistent questions regarding the categorization of music as chutney, several musicians speculated that the name (connoting "hotness") was used initially as a marketing tactic.

One of the first performers acknowledged as being a chutney singer was Sundar Popo who himself claims to have originated the genre. He first used the term "chutney" in 1973. His claim can be seen as a particular kind of historical representation in which he emerges, by virtue of his own testimony, as a "founding father" of a popular music. From Myers' (1984) account of her fieldwork in the 1970s we learnt that the term "chutney" appeared in wedding contexts. Manuel (1998) also notes that the term was in use before Popo would have claimed it as his own in the early 1970s. In the musical biographies of one of the popular genre's foremost performers, however, the link between wedding ritual and chutney is strengthened for Popo's early musical training took the form of attending wedding rituals:

My father is a musician. He is a *tassa* man. When I was very small, most of the time on Friday or Saturday night, they [both his parents] were going to weddings to play *tassa*. My mother had a group of ladies who used to sing at the farewell night [part of the wedding ceremony]. As young children, they couldn't leave us home so they took us with them . . . when you are small and you go – Indian music and melody – we've grown with that. (Sundar Popo, personal interview, 1996)[7]

Another chutney singer, Terry Gajraj, related how he first introduced the word "maticore" [*mathkor*] into his songs,

just to get that word out there. Maticore was something totally different . . . that Friday night thing [taps rhythm: see Score 4.1], you know, that beat there. It's such a simple beat and people used to laugh at it – oh, she doesn't know [how] to play the drums, that's why they [the women] play like that. It was an infectious rhythm and I just decided to try something. (Personal interview, 1996)[8]

Terry Gajraj uses various repeated rhythmic patterns in "maticore mix".

Score 4.1: Examples of maticore rhythms given by Terry Gajraj

According to Sundar Popo, the distinguishing feature of chutney as opposed to soca or chutney soca, for example, is instrumental timbre. The instruments which are typically played in a chutney song are the *dholak*, *dhantal* and harmonium. At least the *dholak* and *dhantal* are also commonly played by women at *mathkor*. These instrumental timbres (particularly the combination of all three) denote "Indianness" even in the context of chutney singers performing old calypso favourites (as Terry Gajraj has done; personal interview, 1996) and in calypsonians' treatments of "Indian" themes (see an example from Mighty Sparrow's *Marajhin*, p. 108).

In terms of musical differences between *mathkor* and chutney songs, musicians mainly referred to rhythm and speed. But while chutney songs are distinguished by their "fast tempo" (Sundar Popo, personal interview, 1996), they draw upon those sections of the *mathkor* ceremony in which the music became more animated to encourage the dancers (Rawatie Ali, personal interview, 1996). The focus on female rather than male dancing at chutney events provides another link between *mathkor* and chutney, especially in view of their choreographic similarities.[9]

One can analyse assertions about chutney's origins in wedding rituals and the contrast in the reception of both forms in terms of gender roles and asymmetries. *Mathkor* dancing is accepted for it serves a functional purpose and is performed within restricted parameters: in private and amongst women. If men are not forbidden to participate in *mathkor*, modesty nevertheless requires that they divert their gaze from the dancing women (as evident from Baloon's statement above). In chutney dancing the focus is on the public, as opposed to private, display of the female body. Chutney as public performance is deemed by many to be unacceptable because it makes public what should be private. What is being made public is not only the dancing but also a challenge to the traditional view of intergender relations amongst Indian-Caribbean people. The dancing indicates the male Hindu's loss of control over the sexuality of the Hindu female, for when she dances "she states emphatically that [her] body and sexuality belong to [her]", thus challenging "one of the most fundamental forms of control of Indian women by Indian men" (Baksh-Soodeen 1991, 7). Responses to this public display have verged on the "hysterical", in the "call for police control over the dancing of Indian women at the chutney festivals [made, for example, by representatives of the Hindu Women's Association]" (Baksh-Soodeen 1991, 7).

The challenge to male authority is made by singing chutney too. Although male chutney singers seem to have appropriated songs that were linked formerly with women's repertoire, there are many female performers who have entered the arena of public performance. Drupatee was one of the first female singers to do so, during the late 1980s. She is known as a calypso and as a chutney singer. Her musical activities point to musical interaction despite the boundaries posited between musics and ethnic groups in Trinidad. As an Indian housewife, Drupatee crossed one kind of social space by entering public performance, and another by intruding, along with other female calypsonians, "into what is virtually a black man's territory" (Warner 1993, 275). So contemporary chutney has much in common with calypso and is described as the "Indian calypso". Musical categorizations are further complicated by the relation of soca to calypso and to chutney. Soca music is regarded by some as being an offshoot of calypso (a combination of African-American soul and calypso) and by others, of chutney (or the Indian-Caribbean forms which are now encompassed by chutney). Ras Shorty I (formerly Lord Shorty), who played a leading role in early performances of soca, apparently intended the word to be spelled "sokah", indicating the Indian influence, especially with regard to *dholak* drumming (Zeno Obi Constance, personal interview, 1996; see also Dudley 1996, 286–87).[10]

While Myers wrote about "a conspicuous absence of acculturation between East Indian and Creole music" (1980, 150), the description of chutney as the "Indian calypso" points to musical interaction. Indeed, Drupatee's well-known calypso recording, "Mr Bissessar" (1988), which featured *tassa* drums so prominently and can thus be regarded as a chutney song indebted to wedding ritual practice, is said to have captured "the growing interpenetration of black/Creole and Indian music" (Warner 1993, 287). Having focused so far on the role of women in *mathkor* and in chutney, the following exploration of the description of chutney as the "Indian calypso" leads us into the minefield of interethnic relations in Trinidad and uncovers further reasons for the controversies surrounding public performance of chutney. The historical representation of chutney's origins in *mathkor* has as much to do with interethnic interaction as it has with gender roles and stylistic similarities.

## INTERETHNIC INTERACTION

Ethnicity in Trinidad "permeates all of the society's social, cultural, political and economic institutions and practices because ethnicity is implicated in the power struggles of everyday life" (Yelvington 1993, 1). This is apparent in the relation between chutney and calypso and in the designation of chutney as the "Indian calypso".

Ribeiro suggests that chutney dancing represents male loss of control over female sexuality amongst Indian-Trinidadians (although some women, such as those active in the Hindu Women's Association, object equally violently to this popular genre). If Ribeiro's suggestion is true, then the creation of an Indian calypso space indicates an attempt to impose some boundaries on that display of sexuality on the basis of ethnicity. According to many commentators, carnival and calypso seemed to be attracting Indian followers who wished to participate in "wining".

Chutney shows provided an alternative where Indian women could interact with other Indians and "wine" as they would at carnival or calypso events. So if some women now express their sexuality more freely through public performance of chutney, it is an expression contained within specified public spaces in which considerations of interethnic interaction play a significant role. It is in this sense that chutney is described as the "Indian calypso", quite apart from considerations of musical similarities.

Such a motivation for the encouragement of female participation in chutney rather than in carnival – "the avoidance of the creolization of Indian women", as one woman told me – stems from the period of indentureship.[11] For most of this period there was little social interaction between Indians and non-Indians. We have already seen how Indian men were reluctant to form alliances with non-Indian women. In the case of women, "parents usually disinherited their daughters or evicted them if they consorted with an African" (Ali 1995, 14). With such attitudes, the traditional view of the Indian woman as docile and submissive became "coupled with that of the Indians as a people who wanted to preserve ethnic purity and were totally against its violation, especially via the marriage or sexual cohabitation of Indian women and Creole men" (Ali 1995, 14). The restrictions on interethnic interaction were reinforced by "a pervasive pattern of residential and occupational segregation. Indians were concentrated on the plantations and in rural settlements, Creoles were in the towns or semi-urban areas" (Brereton 1993, 51–52). Such patterns persist. Clarke examined social interaction between the ethnic groups "East Indian" and "Creole" in south Trinidad by focusing on intermarriage during the period 1960–1980. His data showed small increases in urban exogamy by ethnic categorization while the established pattern of Indian rural endogamy had scarcely changed (Clarke 1993).

While the issue of interethnic interaction, particularly concern over the relationship between the Indian woman and the African man, informs the rise in the popularity of chutney, this is a relationship which has also been extensively explored by calypsonians (for example, Sankar, Melody, Dictator, Lord Shorty, Ebony and Mighty Sparrow; see Constance 1991, chapter 3). Early calypsos (from the 1930s) as well as more recent ones depict the Indian woman as unattainable and describe the objections made by the family against the union of the Indian woman with the African man (in these cases, the calypsonian). Mighty Sparrow's "Marajhin" (1992) provides an example: "When I see you in your *sari* and your *ohrni* [head scarf], I am captivated by your innovative beauty. If it wasn't for your *nanee* [maternal grandmother] and your *bhowji* [sister-in-law], I would marry you and take you in the country."

Some calypso texts explored further the tensions between "Africans" and "Indians". If fears have been voiced regarding the creolization of Indian women in debates about chutney, similar fears were also expressed in calypso song texts of the 1940s and 1950s. In these texts the Indian woman is not always so distant. Constance notes that by the 1950s, calypsonians demonstrated a greater awareness of the Indian presence. In fact, the calypsonian, he suggests "began to see the Indian as an intrusion into his world" (1991, 7). Such an intrusion took form in what was seen as a process of creolization. Thus the calypsonian Killer sang "Indian People with Creole Names" (1951):

> . . . Long ago you see ah Indian by the road
> with his *capra* [cotton suit] waiting to tote people load
> But there is no more Indian again
> Since the women and them take away the Creole names.

This extract reveals particular perceptions of the Indians: as people discarding traditional practices, adopting Creole names and entering different social spaces. If chutney can be analysed in terms of demarcating performance spaces in attempts to avoid the creolization of Indian women, such processes of creolization are (or were) also seen as a threat by the African-Trinidadian population. According to Constance's analysis:

in the 50s it is obvious that calypsonians and by extension the African popu-lace saw these first movements of the East Indian towards creolisation and urbanisation as a threat, a threat to his control of a situation which in fact he only believed he controlled, a threat to his world, to his economic dominance. (1991, 8)

Yelvington's (1993, 1) statement that ethnicity in Trinidad is implicated in the power struggles of everyday life is apparent in these song texts.

While *mathkor* is a Hindu ritual in which women performed within the parameters of a mostly female audience consisting of family members and friends, chutney events allow for a similar performance style in which the parameters delimiting audience have been stretched. Although

**115**

chutney's rise can be accounted for as an attempt to provide an exclusively "Indian" alternative to calypso, this popular genre is becoming as national in character as steelband, carnival and calypso. In fact chutney now attracts a much more (ethnically) diverse audience. Indian female sexuality – as expressed through dance – is put on display for all sectors of the population, and this fuels objections to chutney as part of popular culture. Chutney has not remained an exclusively Indian popular form. By its inclusion (a prominent one at that) in the 1996 carnival celebrations, chutney finally seemed to have gained "national acceptance" (Ribeiro, personal interview, 1996). This coincided with the acceptance of Indian-Trinidadian political leadership. By the mid 1990s, the term "Indian calypso" was, therefore, already in the process of being redefined.

The issue of ethnic identity – though a significant concern for those who disapprove of chutney – has been mitigated by factors of class and residential status. Women who participate in chutney dancing, or even in chutney singing, are described as being low or working class from rural areas (for example, see Baksh-Soodeen 1991, 7; Ribeiro 1992, 45) although no statistical data seem to be available in support of such claims. Value judgements play a role in forming such assumptions. First, such a perception may stem from the somewhat disparaging view of the "folk" and their music, evident in much music scholarship in Trinidad. "Indian music which Trinidadians call authentic Indian classical music," writes Samlal, "is not really so but is *merely* Indian folk music" (1972, 1, emphasis mine). Bissoondialsingh suggests that "against the background of hardships" during the period of indentureship, "what could be expected out of their musical forms but folk music" (1973, 42), music for which "no skills whatsoever are required for its production" (Ramaya 1990, 2). So folk traditions, and hence the popular genres, like chutney, which have grown out of them, are compared unfavourably to other forms, notably to Indian classical music. A second factor that may account for the perception that class and residential status determine who participates in chutney lies in the (unstated) wish to disassociate Indian-Trinidadian women in general with the performance of chutney. Thus, despite the apparent lack of statistical data, in Baksh-Soodeen's (1991) and Ribeiro's (1992) arguments, only certain categories of women, who are rural and working class, are seen as participants in the public performance of chutney.

Those who sing and dance at chutney events are not socially marginalized as are the *shikhat*. The *shikhat* are Moroccan female performers who also publicize, through dance and song, "the intimacies of private life in the public space of ritual and secular celebration" (Kapchan 1994, 82). Chutney dancing however, as it occurs in public performance spaces, is still a contested dance form; it is "vulgar", "inelegant" and indicates some "loss of self-control", "the women just can't help dancing as soon as they hear those drums" and therefore chutney is (or should be) unsuited to the tastes of those of higher social status. But like the *shikhat* who "are threatening precisely because they extend the license of public performance to their private lives as well" (Kapchan 1994, 90), those who protest strongly against chutney performances, such as representatives of the Hindu Women's Association, claim that these performances lead to the breakdown in family life and encourage the development of extra-marital relationships.

Linking chutney to rural women serves to strengthen the historical representation of chutney's origins in *mathkor*. If rural women now predominate at chutney events, they used to do so in the performance of folksongs and dances. Fears that family structures are affected by trends in popular culture offer an interesting perspective on this representation. If chutney is leading to a breakdown of family structures, *mathkor* was (and still is), by contrast, a ceremony in which the extension of kinship through marriage (and, in other similar rituals through the birth of a child) was (and continues to be) celebrated.

The historical representation of chutney's origins in *mathkor* is made by different commentators to support diverse viewpoints. It is more than simply a commentary on the musical genealogy of a contemporary popular genre. Such a representation is made in relation to a variety of complex issues, including those on which I have focused here: gender, ethnicity and social status. Broadly, two contrasting themes emerge from this discussion. It is on one hand a representation which legitimizes chutney as an "Indian" cultural activity for it originates from more ancient traditions which can be traced back to India. From this perspective, any transformations of ritual and folk traditions are cultural developments to be expected. Tracing chutney to a ritual context strengthens its ties to Indian forms rather than to other Caribbean popular genres. As such, chutney can be viewed either as a specifically Indian contribution to Caribbean popular culture or in terms of the preservation and development of tradition in a diasporic context. On the other hand, chutney is perceived as being a desecration of important Hindu rituals, which holds serious consequences. Where *mathkor* has marked the perpetuation of a traditional Indian family structure in Trinidad for over a century, the inappropriate use of music and dance from the ceremony in other contexts, especially public ones, is leading to a breakdown of that structure. The kind of behaviour (particularly that of women) displayed at public performances of chutney has provoked strong criticism.

Accounts that associate Hindu wedding ritual with the popular genre, chutney, are historical representations that have been shaped by, and draw on, the experiences of Indians in the Caribbean. The legacy of indentureship, intergender and interethnic relations are all issues that are evoked, in addition to perceptions of musical and stylistic similarities or differences, by these accounts. The historical representation – *mathkor* to chutney – tells us much about social interactions at a local level.

Although chutney can be understood as a transformation of *mathkor*, such accounts are incomplete in that they pay scant attention, if any, to the diverse sources which have contributed to the development of this contemporary popular genre. Yelvington's argument that in spite of cultural distance between ethnic groups in nineteenth century Trinidad, "syncretisms and acts of cultural borrowing were occurring in the formation of what are seen today as typical Trinidadian forms, such as religion, carnival, calypso and steelband" (1993, 11), holds true in the case of chutney too. While historical representations of chutney link this genre to a homeland in India, the kinds of cultural borrowings or musical exchanges evident in chutney place it in the Caribbean or indeed in the Indian-Caribbean diaspora. In these contexts, these borrowings are musical references read in relation to the workings of gender, social and ethnic categories, and they contribute to the shaping and promotion of this popular genre as another national, cultural form.

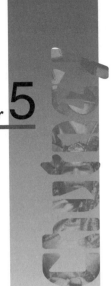

# Chapter 5

# Musical Spaces, Cultural Spaces, Social Spaces

Culture is as much discovery as it is invention and imagination.
— Ramesh Deosaran

The recovery of the past is a feature of shaping postcolonial identities and claims about chutney history can be read in relation to such political projects. In this chapter I will engage therefore, with reflections on postcoloniality in terms of condition (the emergence and construction of new subjectivities) and moment ("postcolonial" as a temporal frame), to interpret the assertion of new kinds of music histories in debates about chutney.

Beginning this book with Captain Angel's account from the context of colonial encounter reminds us that a discussion of music in a postcolonial context refers to ideological orientations as much as to a historical stage (Mishra and Hodge 1993 [1991], 284).[1] His citation of Kipling's sentiment, "never the twain shall meet", is echoed in resistance rhetoric. The Martiniquan writer, Aimé Césaire, for example, in his essay *Discourse on Colonialism* (1993 [1950]) sees only separation, but his view of the gulf between colonized and colonizer is not based on the notions of inherent differences that are apparent in Angel's commentary. "Has colonization really placed civilizations in contact?" asks Césaire (p. 173). His answer is negative: "Between colonizer and colonized there is room only for forced labour, intimidation, pressure, the police, taxation, theft, rape, compulsory crops, contempt, mistrust . . . No human contact, but relations of domination and submission" (p. 177). A meeting point under conditions of colonial contact nevertheless emerges in Césaire's argument for he suggests that the colonizer is decivilized at the same time that the colonized loses civilization.

## HISTORIES AND POSTCOLONIAL DISCOURSES

Ideas about the loss of civilization have been increasingly replaced by the reclamation of history and culture in postcolonial discourses. Yet the postcolonial experience is not a uniform one and there is an ambiguity in the "post" of "postcolonial" which allows as many readings of the term as there are postcolonialisms. "Post-" betrays the lingering effects of the colonial experience. It is also a statement of a politics of resistance and opposition as well as an assertion and expression of experience in which it is now the "colonial" that occupies marginal, peripheral spaces.

Attempting to trace some of chutney's musical elements to India points to the preservation of tradition in a diasporic context. In drawing upon musical ideas from diverse sources, however, chutney can also be interpreted within the paradigm of Caribbean hybridity and fragmentation, which has been so easy to take as a model of, or metaphor for, many postcolonial experiences. The emphasis in the anthropological literature has been on Indians as preservers of culture in Trinidad and hence distinct from other Caribbean populations that have "lost" culture. In a recent survey of Caribbean musics, Manuel (1995) similarly treats Indian-Caribbean music as distinct in a chapter entitled "The Other Caribbean". Such representations of Indians in the Caribbean as people who succeeded in "retaining culture" are compromised by the profound historiographical and methodological problems encountered in attempting to trace the development of chutney. This has been due to the paucity of written accounts and early sound recordings, inconsistencies in oral testimonies, musical change and stylistic diversity – the various kinds of songs that are labelled "chutney".

The Caribbean poet and playwright Derek Walcott writes about a "shattered history", which is applicable to the history of chutney for it is in some ways divorced from the history of Indian music. "Break a vase", he writes and the love that reassembles the fragments is stronger than that love which took its symmetry for granted when it was whole. The glue that fits the pieces is the sealing of its original shape. It is such a love that reassembles our African and Asiatic fragments, the cracked heirlooms whose restoration shows its white scars. (1992, 27)[2]

Walcott's expression, "white scars" is somewhat pejorative. It indicates an inflicted, unwanted or accidental rupture, the breaking of historical threads under colonial rule that cannot be fully restored. For Manuel those white scars are nearly invisible. He comments that "most of Trinidad's musical vitality and cultural dynamism has developed in spite of rather than because of British rule" (1995, 184). Chutney certainly has been held up as a specifically Indian-Caribbean genre and as a marker of an Indian-Caribbean identity. Yet revealing those seemingly fading scars is essential to analysing chutney as a postcolonial public performance genre. The "scars" are visible enough, Sundar Popo sings "phoulourie bina chutney" [a spicy snack without chutney] alongside "Jack and Jill went up the hill to fetch a pail of water", and in terms of instrumentation, the traditional chutney ensemble consists of *dholak*, *dhantal* and harmonium, constituting a soundworld of timbres which are respectively associated with India, the Caribbean and Europe.

## LOCAL COMMENTARIES, LOCAL CULTURE

I shall explore some local commentaries on chutney (presented as case studies) to explore how debates about this genre are linked to wider questions about culture, particularly in relation to forging both national and postcolonial sensibilities. The commentaries have been selected from musicians who have contributed significantly to the performance and development of Indian-Caribbean music (not chutney, but other diverse genres). They hold strong views on the emergence of chutney as Indian-Caribbean music and as part of popular culture. Their commentaries express a sense of duality: of chutney as "Indian" music and as "Caribbean" music. Their views are contradictory. All the commentators demonstrate a sense of negotiating their statements in adopting different perspectives on this subject.

## Case Study 1: A Commentary by Ramaya

In his paper, "Chutney Singing: Its Origin and Development in Trinidad and Tobago", Narsaloo Ramaya (1990) writes that chutney "has suddenly been precipitated in our midst with a devastation unprecedented in the annals of Indian music" (p. 1). Like many other commentators, Ramaya locates the origins of the popular genre, chutney, in wedding music. His paper is interesting because it offers several contrasting judgements of value. He begins his argument by drawing attention to the commercial aspects of music-making and of the financial lures offered by participation in the production of chutney:

The sudden rise of chutney and the regular competitions with fantastic money prizes have rallied the artistes of the country to the call of the money dragon as they fiercely compete with one another for the ultimate prize. Even our respected classical singers have descended into this splurge. They have discarded their polite preoccupation with refined classical singing and are inexorably drawn into the vortex of the new passion of chutney soca. Audience participation now becomes a wild frenzy of pelvic gyrations in which the people have thrown modesty and self-respect to the winds, with mass dancing of unrestrained vulgarity, a spectacle that can fittingly be described as *cultural demolition*. (emphasis mine)

These are, as Ramaya himself notes, "harsh words indeed" and they are used to describe what he perceives as being "a degenerative trend in Indian music" (p. 2).

Ramaya's portrayal of cultural demolition stems from his view that chutney is "Indian" music. It is drawn, too, by the distinction he makes between past and present musical activities. Music, he suggests, provided some comfort to the disillusioned and disappointed indentured labourers who arrived in Trinidad:

In this situation they found comfort and sustenance in their culture – their music and song, their rituals and festivals. The singing of *Tulsidas chowpaies* [songs or poems of four lines] and Kabir's *bhajans* were comforting after the day's toil and the throwing of *abeer* [coloured water thrown at the *phagwa* festival], the beating of *tassa* drums and dancing the fire-pass were the beginning of their cultural practices. They were the pioneers who sang the first *sohars* [songs sung to celebrate the birth of a child] and *launis* [women's songs about the absence of husbands at work], the *biraha* and *chowtal* [usually praises of Krishna sung at the spring festival of *phagwa*], *hori* [classical song] and *chaiti* [*chatti*, the celebration which takes place six days after the birth of a child], *marsuyas* [*marsiyas*, sung by women at *Hosay* processions] and *bhajans* . . . Unlike our vibrant electrifying chutney songs today the early folk songs were simple melodies, lullabies and chants reflecting the simple life of the estate workers, their homely joys and sorrows, their festivals and rituals, their work ways, their manners, customs and ceremonies. (Ramaya 1990, 4)

If chutney is described at the outset as a "degenerative trend", Ramaya's comments become more favourable as he considers the reception of the genre in India and cultural exchanges between India and Trinidad. In these exchanges, chutney is seen as being specifically Indian-Caribbean – not just a degenerative trend in Indian music but a form which displays local (Caribbean) musical innovations:

Visiting artistes from India have been fascinated by the unique style of our songs . . . to the extent that they have taken entire songs with lyrics and music and carried them away to India to tantalize and titillate their folks back home. They then send them back with slight variation to Trinidad. There is a strange irony in this, not unlike the mercantile practice of Imperial Britain of colonial times taking our raw sugar to England and exporting it back to Trinidad in the form of refined granulated sugar, for indeed the many and varied original folk songs that were brought here, crude and unembellished as they were, became a rich medium for the development of our talents . . . Kanchan, a leading playback pop singer of the Indian movies aroused audiences in India with the exciting swing and rhythm of our music . . . What a paradox, what an incongruous irony to see the master become the student, the guru the *chela*, the *ustad* the *shagird*. (Ramaya 1990, 9)

The apparent contradictions in his appraisal of chutney are partly reconciled in the concluding statements. However, the status of chutney as "Indian" or as Indian-Caribbean remains unresolved. Despite drawing attention to musical hybridity, chutney has the potential, according to Ramaya, to contribute to "Indian" music:

We feel proud to be the inheritors of this [Indian] culture and prouder still to be able to use this culture as a foundation upon which to formulate our own interpretation of India's ancient art . . . Chutney is part of this metamorphosis, the hybrid offspring of our musical heritage . . . Chutney shorn of its lewdness and vulgarity can become one of the most stimulating innovations in Indian music. (Ramaya 1990, 10)

## Case Study 2: A Commentary by Patasar

The romanticized depiction of indentured labourers participating in folk music activities is a common one. Patasar's construction of the musical activities of the indentured labourers is similar to Ramaya's in his emphasis on folk traditions being performed as part of everyday life:

Our forefathers woke up at four in the morning which was the Brahm Mahurta or auspicious hour, with a song on their lips in praise of the Lord. While taking their baths they recited another mantra *"om Ganga cha Yamuna"* [praise be to Ganga and also to Yamuna]. After their baths they sat for prayers which were all recited in song. On their way to the fields they sang special songs. Depending on the type of work in which they were involved, there were always appropriate songs. A fisherman had his particular repertoire, so too did the weaver, the cobbler, and the ladies who sang *"loories"* [lullabies] to put their babies to sleep at home. They also sang songs while waiting for their husbands. (Patasar 1995, 77)

Mungal Patasar is famous in Trinidad for his experiments in fusing different musical traditions, for example, combining steel pan and *sitar*. Since chutney is a genre which draws on diverse musical traditions it seems to point to the kind of musical interaction that Patasar encourages and develops in his own musical activities. Yet Patasar (1995), like Ramaya, is critical of what he describes as being a "highly commercial venture" which is "pointing Indian music in a new direction" (p. 82). He regards chutney as being a popular adaptation of Indian folk music, but one that has "flaws" because of the regurgitation of a few tunes and the inappropriate use of religious song texts: "It is limited to very few tunes, the lyrics are the words of bhajans or religious songs and the singers themselves are hopeless in the area of creating new tunes" (p. 82). Furthermore, chutney emerges in Patasar's analysis as a site of cultural contestation. He speaks of the promotion of the genre as a "weapon" against "Indian" culture:

The people who propagate chutney as the only form of Indian music in Trinidad are the greatest antagonists of the true development of our music. In this case the word "Indigenous" is used as a fad, as a weapon against Indian culture. The blurring of discrete cultural space continues, masquerades, as "multiculturalism. (p. 85)

If chutney has flaws according to Patasar's view, folk music itself "remains almost motionless as it is linked to a few tunes that keep recurring with increasing rhythm" (Patasar 1995, 83). Patasar suggests that musical stagnation characterizes both folk and popular genres and concludes that this is evidence of "cultural atrophy". Chutney, he argues, "can only move in one direction and that is the direction of calypso. The modern structure of chutney is an evolution towards the more aggressive calypso. This in itself is not a problem. The predicament is that in the final analysis it would be lost just as the local classical music was when it gave way to chutney" (p. 83). In this statement we see concern for the potential loss of "Indian" musical expressions, where to be "Indian" is significant in the local, Caribbean context. Hence the comparison between chutney and calypso. While he is worried that chutney's Indian characteristics will be lost by the incorporation of ideas from calypso, he is concerned, too, that the chutney tradition should not be a static one. Atrophy stems from focusing on the preservation of a folk repertoire rather than creatively experimenting with musical ideas.

If Patasar is critical of the exchange of musical ideas between chutney and calypso he nevertheless advocates such exchanges, albeit with alternative musical genres, as the basis for future developments. Like Ramaya, he holds definite views about the direction which chutney should take. His recommendations ultimately serve local, not Indian, interests. While deriding the influence of calypso, he is equally unenamoured about the influence of Indian film music:

Chutney music emanates from the heart of a people fighting for a chance to express themselves in a way that would be universally accepted. It is presently in the hands of the folk and it maintains the character of the folk. The development of this art form is therefore vital to the people of this nation. But the vision of the people who propagate it is limited . . . My submission is that the Raaga system and the European harmony should be its base. In this way we could throw off the shackles of dependency on filmi [Indian film] music and create something indigenous to our own experience as citizens of this land. (Patasar 1995, 83)

## Case Study 3: A Commentary by Maharaj

While many scholarly activities and local debates have focused on folk traditions and on the notion that these were the traditions that were maintained in diasporic contexts, less attention has been paid to classical traditions. Indeed, Myers claims that "Indian classical music was introduced to the island [Trinidad] in 1966" (1984, 5) with the arrival of

Professor Adesh who arrived as a representative of the Indian Council for Cultural Relations in New Delhi, India. While most local commentators argue that knowledge of classical traditions existed during the indentureship period, they remain relatively uninvestigated. A noteworthy exception is Shivannand Maharaj's thesis (1994). Like Helen Myers, Maharaj's view of Indian classical traditions in Trinidad has been shaped by an involvement with Professor Adesh (in this case as one of Adesh's students). Maharaj proposes a two-part model, differentiating between Indian classical music in Trinidad from 1845 to the present (labelled type A) and from the 1960s to the present (type B). Thus far the model is straightforward in that it follows commonly held perceptions of the history of Indian classical music in the Caribbean. Maharaj continues by describing the distinctions between types A and B. The differences he outlines accord with Ramaya's perceptions of the relation between past and present and, indeed, Maharaj refers to Ramaya's work extensively. Type A is described as follows: "its nature is more folk-oriented and the musical forms in terms of melody and rhythm are different to type B". By contrast, classical music, which is placed under type B "is highly systematised. It is studied formally from books and practical training is provided by Gurus who have mastered this art" (Maharaj 1994, 5).

Chutney is accommodated under type A in Maharaj's thesis: "type A classical is popularly known as "tent singing". This formed the major part of the entertainment on the night before an Indian wedding" (1994, 28). By typifying this repertoire as "classical", Maharaj is also able to enter the debate about the value and influence of chutney. He comments:

With the type A classical, many of the singers interviewed [for his study] expressed their anger towards the media promoters. They were of the opinion that classical music has been suppressed by these very people, who promoted more chutney music for their personal gains . . . [His interviewees] see a grim future ahead and are outraged at the severe damage done to classical music by chutney singing. (pp. 31–32)

## CHUTNEY HISTORIES, CONTESTED SITES

Revisions, reclamations or reinventions in music histories of chutney are not just preoccupations with the past but visions for the future. Political unity and musical interactions as a vehicle for expressing a national coherence retain their significance. However, contrapuntal assertions of specific and distinctive experiences, ethnicities and identities within the independent nation also clamour for attention. It is one of the contradictions of debates about the role of chutney in Trinidad that some of the most vociferous contributors have been cultural activists who are musicians but not chutney practitioners. Discarding or at least reweaving the colonial mantle is one part of their visions for the future of chutney. This project, however, is intertwined with assessments of the kinds of musical dialogues that had been initially encouraged by the meeting of musics in colonial Trinidad.

Ramaya (1990) provides an example of the marginalization of the "colonial" through drawing on other histories which either do not anticipate or else negate the impact of the colonial era. His assessment of chutney is not entirely positive. For him it is "a spectacle that can fittingly be described as cultural demolition" for it is a "degenerative trend in Indian music" (p. 2). Despite this portrayal of cultural demolition, chutney for Ramaya is one of those Indian-Caribbean interpretations of "India's ancient art" (p. 2) and therefore, as the "hybrid offspring of our [Trinidadian] musical heritage", it has the potential to "become one of the most stimulating innovations in Indian music" (p. 10). Looking back to an ancient past and evaluating chutney in relation to Indian music can be read as a way of displacing a colonial displacement. But this is one reading of Ramaya. In thinking about the postcolonial, the colonial intrudes, whatever the attempts to overlook its presence.

Chutney as a "hybrid offspring" offers a reminder, too, of a colonial heritage which has left particular legacies of musical dialogues and which demands some kind of response to them. Patasar, who also writes about chutney in relation to "Indian" music, is thus able to argue at the same time that the development of chutney is vital to the people of Trinidad. In his description, the promotion of chutney as representative of Indian music is presented as a weapon against "Indian" culture and what he sees as the musical stagnation of the genre is evidence of "cultural atrophy". For him, chutney can only move in the direction of the calypso that would lead to the loss of Indian musical elements. While Patasar is critical of the exchange of musical ideas between chutney and calypso, he nevertheless advocates such exchanges, albeit with alternative models, as the basis for future developments. Like Ramaya, he holds definite views about the direction that chutney should take. Equally unenamoured with the influence of Indian film music as he is with that of calypso, he recommends that the raaga system and European harmony should be the base for chutney in creating something "indigenous" (Patasar 1995, 830). Those "white scars" are still visible. The glue that holds together the pieces of the broken vase, of which Walcott writes, cannot restore it to its original shape.

Some chutney histories, however, have displaced the colonial displacement more forcibly than Ramaya has done in his evaluative text or than Patasar in his suggestions for the musical development of chutney. This is perhaps best illustrated by the central historical representation of chutney (made by practitioners, audiences and critics alike) as a development of music and dance from ceremonies such as *mathkor*, and thereby linking this contemporary popular music with Indian ritual practice.

The commentaries outlined here provide glimpses into intellectual historical reconstructions and projections of Indian music in Trinidad. The analyses are made by musicians and cultural activists who have immediate interests in the presentation, representation and development of contemporary Indian-Trinidadian musical practice. While there are similarities between these accounts in terms of the emphasis on folk-oriented traditions as the inheritance of the descendants of the indentured labourers and the location of chutney's origins in those traditions, there is also much individual variation. All the accounts present contradictory appraisals of chutney. For Maharaj, for example, chutney is classified in a category of classical music, but his evaluations of the genre point to the damage it inflicts on classical music in Trinidad. By other commentators cited here, chutney is perceived on one hand as a flawed tradition, "a negative development", "a degenerative trend", and its effects on Indian culture in the Caribbean have been devastating with claims being made about "cultural demolition" and "cultural atrophy". On the other hand, chutney provides evidence of local creativity. It stems from the central repertory of Indian-Trinidadian music (the wedding and birth songs) and it has the potential to be "one of the most stimulating innovations in Indian music". Its development in Trinidad is vital since it provides a medium whereby local musicians may "create something indigenous to our own experiences as citizens of this land". The contradictions in these statements are perhaps vital in thinking about chutney in relation to postcolonial thought, for they point to different subject positions (no single native mind here) and to the playing out of other kinds of current contestations. In presenting their views on, and value judgements of, chutney these commentators are also claiming rights to represent a popular music in ways that they believe are appropriate. Their statements, then, cannot be dismissed.

That chutney is analysed in the accounts outlined above in relation to calypso and carnival in Trinidad, adding to local debates about cultural and social as well as musical spaces, is indicative of a history of interaction and separation between "Indians" and "Africans" extending into the present from the indentureship period. Current debates are similar to past ones. Cultural spaces are contested sites where weapons are literal and not just metaphorical. John Cowley's examination, for example, of nineteenth century newspaper articles shows that Africans and Indians participated in both *canboulay* and *Hosay* processions [a Muslim festival] as early as the 1850s (1996, 84). But such commonality was cause for concern on the part of colonial authorities. Both the *Hosay* procession and *canboulay* involved marching through the streets with lighted torches, which in 1881 became reason enough for police interference and the suppression of *canboulay*. The effects of this action had serious ramifications for *Hosay* activities. Motivated by fears of "joint insurrection by black Creoles and East Indians", the *Port of Spain Gazette* (1 March 1881) called for the festival to be held only on plantation areas thereby segregating the Indians and the Creoles. Such regulations, issued in 1884, which confined the festival to plantation areas were rejected by Indians, particularly around San Fernando:

On 30 October, therefore, participants chose to disregard the authorities and carry their *tajahs* [model mausoleums for the grandsons of the Prophet Mohammed] towards San Fernando. Police . . . fired a hail of bullets to stop the advance, and this resulted in many deaths. (Cowley 1996, 103)

## NEW HISTORIES? RECONCEPTUALIZING THE PAST

The past has been even further reconceptualized. Believing that Indian classical music was introduced to Trinidad as recently as 1966, Myers asked the guru, Adesh, how it could be that the Indians in the Caribbean had discovered within themselves an instant love for the urban art music of north India, a tradition which seemed to be as foreign to them as to her. He told her, "It is their heredity, their parentage. The link was not broken since they came here. The link wasn't broken. If the link had been broken, then this love could not exist. It would have changed" (Myers 1984, 66).

In making such a statement, Adesh as an Indian classical musician can be seen as promoting his own interests and stressing the relevance of his own practice to Trinidadian audiences. Local musicians have also been keen to find a link with Indian classical traditions (that extends beyond current engagements with them). Mungal Patasar locates a link with Indian classical music in the oral memory:

The classical music of the Indians which was brought here [to Trinidad] may well have Folk origins, but what is certain is that the folk who came here would have been exposed to classical music at an aural level, and would certainly have worked classical elements, consciously or unconsciously, into the Folk music. (Patasar 1995, 79)

In addition to general concepts of *raag* and *taal* and ties to folk traditions, Indian-Caribbean music, according to the historian, Brinsley Samaroo, may have closer connections with Indian classical traditions than hitherto imagined or hoped. These connections centre around the Lucknowi classical tradition which may have been held in the oral memory of some of the migrants. Both folk and classical traditions from India, then, have shaped contemporary popular musical practice (Samaroo 1996). How far can this reconceptualization of the past be substantiated? Nawab Wajid Ali Shah, the King of Avadh (or as named by the British, Oudh) is a central figure in this history of chutney. In his Lucknow court, musicians exerted a tremendous influence. In fact, the court of the nawabs of Avadh in Lucknow had been one of the most important centres for musical patronage outside of Delhi since the second half of the eighteenth century (Powers 1980, 81). Wajid Ali Shah was deposed in 1856 by British authorities and he moved with his retinue to Calcutta. This city subsequently became a centre for musical activity with musicians moving there in search of potential patrons (Capwell 1993, 97). Wajid Ali Shah played a role in establishing his music and dance school (1856–1887). The school was located next door to the "Coolie Depot" from where Indian migrants boarded the ships that transported them to other parts of the British Empire.

During Wajid Ali Shah's stay in Calcutta and after his death, members of his retinue may have, as Samaroo suggests, migrated to the Caribbean carrying their musical knowledge with them (Samaroo 1996). The reference to the *sitar* as an instrument that indentured labourers took with them to Trinidad (Fazal's testimony in Mahabir's collection, see chapter 2) is interesting in relation to Samaroo's hypothesis for it raises questions about a colonial erasure of histories and local hierarchies. While the *sitar* seems to have been present in Trinidad, it was not widespread in India even by the late nineteenth century. The renowned *sitarist*, Ghulam Raza Khan, was a leading musician in Wajid Ali Shah's court, however, and this centre was important in the development of the instrument.[3] Accounting for the *sitar* in Trinidad presents another challenge to a postcolonial dismantling of the colonialist perception. Since the *sitar* would not be normally associated with nineteenth century Bhojpuri labourers, its presence in the Caribbean context offers a reminder that the social class of "labourer" was a colonial construct. Anyone travelling through the "Coolie Depot", possibly including members of Wajid Ali Shah's court, became "labourers" who would be regarded in relation to their productivity potential on the plantations. Postcolonial critiques in the form of these kinds of histories contribute to the reclamation of the diversity of social backgrounds from which the Indian migrants came.

This story of how Indian classical music is taken to the Caribbean is a possible historical narrative. It can be read as a response to Chakrabarty's question, "Who speaks for 'Indian' pasts?" Dipesh Chakrabarty's aim is to provinicialize a "European" history by exposing the kinds of tales that both imperialism and nationalism have told to the "colonized" and to the "postcolonized". "Indian history," argues Chakrabarty "even in the most dedicated socialist or nationalist hands, remains a mimicry of a certain 'modern' subject of 'European' history and is bound to represent a sad figure of lack and failure. The transition narrative will always remain 'grievously incomplete' " (1997 [1992], 239).

Chakrabarty points to the politics of location in discussing the incompleteness of historical narratives which always present a geographic referent to a relation with Europe. Nevertheless, there is now a growing body of texts on the Indian diasporic experience which offer other perspectives on postcolonial questions. These studies are not laments of that which is incomplete or cannot be retrieved but forays into questions which have been uncovered as legitimate. Viewing indenture as a "new system of slavery" (Wood 1968; Williams 1964 [1962]) and indentured labourers as the victims of colonial projects (Dabydeen and Samaroo 1987) is giving way to more positive ideas about those Indian migrants. The Indian migrants are seen not only as duped victims, but also as enterprising agents, motivated for various economic and personal reasons to seek opportunities elsewhere (Seecharan 1997). The song text about the Bengali Babu who hopes to cross the *kala pani* only to bring wealth back to India (see chapter 2) adds weight to this perspective. It is in this spirit of reassessment that claims being made about chutney's genealogy (women's folk and ritual repertoire and classical traditions) can be interpreted. That this popular music springs from women's repertoire suggests an authentic preservation, for women in this context are seen as tradition-bearers. Classical traditions are important because of the high status that has been accorded to them in Trinidad with their promotion by visiting figures such as Professor Adesh and study trips to India undertaken by some leading Trinidadian performers (including Mungal Patasar). Chutney, then, draws on valued traditions traced to India while simultaneously establishing a musical space identified as "Indian-Caribbean" and "indigenous" to the Caribbean.

While Chakrabarty's critique is aimed at the discipline of history which places Europe at its centre and towards which all historical imagination currently gravitates (Chakrabarty 1997 [1992], 243), Indian diasporic voices complicate this politics of location. The Indian-Trinidadian historical imagination looks towards India, Europe and other diasporas as its heritage and as its pasts. The Indian past is fundamental to a history of chutney and, together with the incorporation of new musical ideas from India, it informs the construction of a Caribbean "Indianness", but it is only one part of the past.

Catherine Hall notes that almost everyone who lives in the Caribbean "has come from somewhere else" (1996, 68), thus rendering possible a recognition of oneself as, for example, African or Indian and diasporized. The testimonies examined above with regard to chutney's history indicate the extent to which Indian-Trinidadians have begun to see themselves as Indians and diasporized. But the debates about "Indianness" are relevant in the Caribbean context. Chutney as a music "indigenous" to Trinidad reveals the need to revise the emphasis on "village India" (Klass 1961) and cultural persistence amongst Indians in the Caribbean (which was criticized by Williams 1962, for whom this view was a continuation of a colonial policy of separation and fragmentation). This is highlighted by a second diaspora that shows people becoming conscious of themselves as Caribbean nationals and diasporized. The image of the ship has been used in telling the story of this diaspora too. The 1998 celebrations of fifty years of Caribbean contributions to Britain focused on the arrival of the Windrush at

Tilbury Docks in 1948. The Trinidadian calypsonian Lord Kitchener was greeted by the British Broadcasting Corporation and on request he sang a calypso marking his arrival in the "mother country", Britain. Since then, chutney, too, has found performance spaces in various centres of the Caribbean diaspora as well as in the World Music market. An Indian past is significant in chutney music histories but it is entangled with the pasts and present of other "motherlands".

## MUSICAL SPACES

The kinds of musical exchanges that appear to have occurred on board the *Sheila* raise questions about the siting of culture and the social and cultural spaces in which musical activity takes place. The *Sheila* was one kind of musical space. Angel's account of that space began to foreground musical hybridity emerging from a hierarchically demarcated context.

A preoccupation with changing musical spaces and their relation to sociocultural spaces is evident in histories of Hindustani music. One famous story, which was narrated to me in Trinidad, concerns Tansen (c. 1500–89) and his guru, Swami Haridass. The story is pertinent here, for Tansen is the almost legendary figure to whom many north Indian musicians, including H. S. Adesh, who has played a role in reviving interest in north Indian classical traditions in Trinidad, trace their musical lineage. The story tells us more about spaces than about history, for the ways in which musical lineages in India are traced leads to much contestation. Tansen became a part of the Mughal musical establishment in 1562 when he joined the court of the Emperor Akbar (Powers 1980, 81). The story is that Emperor Akbar asked Tansen to take him to his guru, Swami Haridass. Akbar was so impressed with Haridass's performance that when he returned to his court, he asked Tansen to sing the same *bhajan* that his guru had sung. Akbar, however, was not so satisfied with Tansen's rendition. Tansen explained that his performance could not be as uplifting for he sang before a king, but his guru sang for God.

In this story, the relationship between Tansen and Haridass can be interpreted as "an expression of that attitude about music in India which alternates at the extremes of considering it sacred activity and everyday entertainment" (Neuman 1990, 85). The musical spaces are those of the temple and of the court, of the sacred and of the secular. Contemporary musicians speak about a third musical space: the international concert

**133**

stage, on which Ravi Shankar has achieved renown. Neuman writes that "where Tansen represents the movement from the temple to the court, Ravi Shankar . . . represents the movement to the concert stage . . . Musicians are, in a sense, now twice removed from the sacred and magical . . . 'It is the common man,' as some musicians are fond of putting it, 'that calls the tune' " (1990, 68). In moving to the international concert stage, the tradition has undergone change. Similarly, chutney in Trinidad is the music of the "common man", as it has become part of popular culture. Traditions from India, in this case, have also moved to different performance, social, and cultural spaces. These traditions have undergone change in the spaces of the Indian diaspora.

My intention here is not to assert that Indian-Caribbean musical traditions can be traced to the Lucknowi classical traditions or even to Tansen. Rather, Tansen's story, the relocation of Wahid Ali Shah from Lucknow to Calcutta, and Ravi Shankar's emergence on the international concert stage throw light on the shifting spaces in which musical activity takes place and accompanying changes to musical traditions. Tansen's performance was not the same as that of his guru, Swami Haridass. Tansen sang before a king and not for God. He introduced sacred music into a public space, the court, and in so doing he established himself as a leading musician in the history of north Indian classical music. There is a parallel here with chutney. If criticism has been levelled at the form for bringing into a public space what should be private, its severest critics have also recognized the potential for chutney to represent an indigenous – Indian-Caribbean – musical tradition on the world stage. Local commentaries appear contradictory, then, because they deal with the juxtaposition of musical spaces (private and public, local and diasporic) and traditions. These dualities, which stem from musical changes which have occurred as a result of the move of people from depots such as the one at Calcutta to the Caribbean, can be compared to those applied to Ravi Shankar in his move to the international arena. Shankar can be perceived as a mediator between a traditional music and modernity (Slawek 1993). He has "often been regarded as nontraditional both by Indians and by non-Indians" because of "his success in creating new contexts for his tradition" (Slawek 1993, 167). These new contexts include the combination of north Indian and Western classical traditions (such as the concertos for *sitar* and orchestra), and experiments with avant-garde, electronic and fusion music (for example, collaborating with the minimalist composer Philip Glass). As well as being criticized for his innovations, however, he has been much admired and has secured audiences for Indian music around the globe. If Shankar has found an Indian musical space in the global context, the rise of chutney as another kind of "transformed tradition", which is performed in new contexts like Trinidad and draws upon musical ideas from calypso, soca and rap, points to the establishment of an Indian musical space in the Caribbean. Retaining the term "chutney" (as in soca chutney) indicates innovation within a tradition instead of the emergence of new genres generated by musical change. Just as Ravi Shankar is respected both for innovative ideas and knowledge of tradition, chutney musicians who compete in the Chutney Monarch contest must perform different types of chutney which are categorized as "original, traditional chutney", sung in both English and Hindi, "open category chutney" and a test piece which is a song composed specifically for the competition.

## INDIAN MUSIC IN THE CARIBBEAN OR INDIAN-CARIBBEAN MUSIC?

Ethnomusicologists turned their attention to processes of musical culture contact during the 1980s, moving away from a focus on local musics with small-scale bounded audiences. Around the same time, the Caribbean became "ethnographically interesting" for anthropologists because it seemed to provide a model for probing processes of globalization and creolization (Mintz 1996). Studies of traditions in Caribbean contexts (such as Herskovits and Herskovits 1947; Klass 1961) thus anticipated a later interest in processes of cultural flow and in cultural preservation and change.

The conceptual vocabulary that has been used in discussions about musical culture contact includes terms like "hybrid, cross-fertilized, pastiche, transplanted, exotic, fused, blended, integrated, osmotic, creole, mestizo, mulatto, syncretic, synthesized, acculturated" (Kartomi 1981, 228). In reacting to ethnomusicological disapproval of such mixed musics, Kartomi suggested that while it may be historically interesting to establish the parentage of a musical culture, emphasis should be placed on the "new music" itself which is "housed in a new social context with its own set of extramusical meanings" (1981, 233). The new music certainly needs to be understood on its own terms, but this view suggests that difference is created between musical traditions because the parent musics remain static in the same social context while the hybridized music changes in a new context. Chutney is a popular Caribbean form which demands consideration of its Indian roots. The practitioners of and audience for chutney stress these historical connections. Yet a history of a musical tradition is not straightforward, as I have shown in relation to chutney. Trying to identify the roots of a tradition in the "parent" music raises further issues about music historiography for the parent musics themselves have undergone processes of "hybridization".

While local commentaries discuss Indian music in the diasporic context, the representation of this music centres around its relevance to Caribbean musical life: "visiting artistes from India have been fascinated by the unique style of our songs" writes Ramaya (1990, 9); and "the development of this art form [chutney] is . . . vital to the people of this nation" claims Patasar (1995, 83). The references made to India are partly due to the sense of historical background, and partly as a result of contemporary interactions with India which occur in increasingly global arenas for musical activity. In this sense, chutney shares important characteristics with many Caribbean musics. It shapes and is shaped by other musics. Guilbault writes with reference to zouk that it "creates much stress in its countries of origin [Martinique, Guadeloupe, St Lucia, Dominica] by underscoring how its relation with the international market reformulates local traditions and creative processes" (1993, 209). Zouk, *son*, salsa (which was a marketing term for Cuban musics used by a record company in New York), calypso and reggae are examples of the myriad Caribbean music forms which have become part of a World Music scene. From traditions that have been fragmented and reformulated, these musics emerge as potent symbols in expressions of specific identities, politics and philosophies.

Whether chutney is represented as "Indian" or as "Indian-Caribbean" music is related to the politics of a cultural displacement. The emergence of chutney in the public space of popular culture challenges the model of Indian-Caribbean people being the preservers of an Indian culture in a new geographic context. As part of Caribbean popular culture, chutney cannot be seen as being just "Indian" music in the Caribbean.

## Musical Dialogues and the "Brotherhood of the Boat"

With regard to contemporary practice, musical interactions extend beyond the triangular framework of the Indian past which is preserved or forgotten, the impact of colonial influence and the Indian-Caribbean experience. The triangle has been recast. Indian-Trinidadians have reclaimed interactions with India which are based as much on exchanges as on receiving and reviving the Indian heritage. They have been profoundly influenced by, and in turn have contributed to, local cultural and social expressions which extend beyond Trinidad to the Caribbean as a region. Chutney is performed in the former colonial centre, the heart of empire, London. In terms of timbre, the use of *dholak*, *dhantal* and harmonium continue to be defining features of chutney, but musicians are just as likely to replace them with programmed drum machines and keyboards, or to add, for example, trumpets, trombones, steelpans and drum-kits. With these additions, the kind of chutney which is produced is often further identified as being soca chutney or ragga chutney. These terms indicate interactions with calypsonians, soca, reggae, ragga and rap musicians and locate chutney in a wider Caribbean context. These musical dialogues are at their most apparent in the club mix and in reworkings of the most popular chutney songs (for example, the collaboration between the chutney singer Sonny Mann, the ragga singer General Grant, and the soca singer Denise Belfon, in a reworked recording of "Loota La", Rituals Label, *Caribbean Party Rhythm* 1, CR3397, 1996).

The club mix is an apt illustration of Deosaran's notion of "interactive diversity":

Cultural relations in this country are not static; they are not irretrievably hooked to racial categories. There is a cultural fluidity that is often ignored . . . Indians as a group are now undergoing more cultural change than other groups in the society . . . There is a process of selective integration within the Indian community itself, that is, they are practising westernised, creolised lifestyles while at the same time retaining their traditional rituals and modes of cultural practices . . . While the exact extent of this within-group integration is yet to be determined empirically, many of the signs are obvious. For example, many East Indians today play Carnival, lavishly join in fast-food and calypso frolic, sing and enjoy non-Indian songs. All this while still enjoying Indian songs and dance, food and clothes. According to Rikki Jai [a calypso/chutney singer], the Indian girl says: "Hold the Lata Mangeshkar [popular Indian film singer], give me soca." Rikki Jai is wrong. The Indian girl likes both . . . What really is "Indian" culture in this country? In the first place, "Indian" culture today in Trinidad is less East Indian and more Trinidadian. The diversity we practice is not a partitioned diversity but an interactive diversity. We therefore have to begin revising those old-fashioned notions about static cultural pluralism and cultural conflict. (Deosaran 1995, 181–82)

*Photo 10: Rikki Jai singing at a chutney show in London (photograph by Suresh Rambaran, reproduced with permission)*

Deosaran's comment and his call for ideological revisions point to shifts in analytical frameworks that are in part a result of sociopolitical changes. In recent depictions of chutney, the model of musical inter-action which focuses on a cultural flow from colonizer to colonized at least has been discarded. The ways in which music can articulate ideologies, conflicts and assertions of difference which framed the colonial project are still evident in recent interpretations of chutney, but a scenario of complex cultural interactions also emerges. So chutney is seen as a medium for the expressions of Indian-Caribbean women in the power struggles that occur in gendered spaces according to Kanhai (1995); as one of the sites in Trinidad in which contestations over local or national culture are played out as argued by Reddock (1995); and in one of my own interpretations, as a marker of Indian-Caribbean identity in the global as well as local arena (see chapter 3). This popular genre, then, is analysed on micro and macro levels by looking at current socio-cultural interactions in local, regional and global contexts. In these analyses, not only has the divisive model of colonizer/colonized been replaced, but the "colonial" itself has become marginalized: a part of history.

In urging for the revision of ideas about cultural conflict, Deosaran's statements can be regarded as a variation on Eric Williams' political rhetoric. Timed to coincide with the eve of Trinidadian independence, Williams' *History of the People of Trinidad and Tobago* appeared on 31 August 1962. It was part of that "colonial nationalist project of the rewriting of the history purveyed by metropolitan scholars" (Williams 1964 [1962], vii). Although Williams was a noted historian as well as statesman (he was prime minister of Trinidad and Tobago from 1961 until his death in 1981), he was aware of the extent to which scholarship is not just the production of knowledge about a subject but a political, discursive practice (a point made by Mohanty 1996 in relation to feminist scholarship). Williams' document was explicitly presented as a political manifesto: "a manifesto of a subjugated people. Designed to appear on Independence Day, August 31, 1962, it is the Declaration of Independence of the united people of Trinidad and Tobago" (p. x).

Williams' vision of unity was expressed in his often quoted concluding remarks that there could be no mother Africa, mother India, mother China, mother Lebanon . . . or mother England for the citizens of Trinidad and Tobago. He saw the postcolonial state as one in which the arts (poetry, music, painting, sculpture and the novel) would flourish (p. 247–48). In a similar reflection on political aspirations and artistic expressions, the current prime minister (Basdeo Panday) has identified the musical dialogues of the songs of the chutney singer, Sonny Mann, as an example of "crossculturalisation of music" which takes "a step in the direction of national unity" (cited by Ramoutar 1996, 8).

Yet the aftermath of emancipation – the victory of a new postcolonial order, the installation of the People's National Movement into political office, and the urgency of the moves towards decolonization – was racked by conflicts of other kinds. These conflicts included social unrest and protests about the socioeconomic conditions of many Trinidadians and the continuing dominance of white representatives in public sectors, the rise of the Black Power movement (with its slogan "Indians and Africans unite now"), antigovernment demonstrations with questions raised about the role of foreign capital within the nation, and politically motivated violence which culminated with the February (carnival time) revolt of 1970. As Bennett notes, when it was perceived that the postcolonial order had not fully led to the anticipated transformation of Trinidad, "radical intellectuals, students, and the urban dispossessed concluded that 'Massa Day no Dun Yet' " (Bennett 1989, 144).[4]

Singers articulate these tensions in complex ways. Their expressions, presented in public forums too, address issues of unity in their song texts at the same time as they are involved in reinventing mother Africa or India or calling for mother Trinidad and Tobago. Bob Marley's example of freedom songs and expressions of pan-African unity (with songs like "Africa Unite", "Zimbabwe", "War", "Exodus") continue to find resonances in Trinidad. In chutney and calypso texts, images of the boat and references to both the middle passage and the other middle passage (the Indian voyage to the Caribbean) are evoked in song narratives. The boat as a focus for a diasporic imagination offers a space for the presentation of two dominant narratives, that of the common Caribbean experience and also the specific journeys undertaken by the diverse peoples who now make up the region. Two such texts by Brother Marvin (example 5.1) and by Sundar Popo were composed for the 1995 Arrival Day celebrations (150 years of Indians in the Caribbean).

## Example 5.1: Brother Marvin's "Jihaji Bhai" ("Brotherhood of the Boat")

I am the seed of me father
He is the seed of me grandfather
Who is the seed of babu kancha
He came from Calcutta
He stick on a bag on his shoulder
He took bag and he *caphra* [cotton suit]
So I am part seed of India.
India.

The Indians came on the ship of slavery
Bind together two races in unity
There was no more mother Africa
No more mother India
Just mother Trini.
My pa who [?] in sugar cane
Down in the Caroni Plain
Ram loga [?]
*Jihaji bhai*, brotherhood of the boat.

*Jihaji bhai*, brotherhood of the boat
*Jihaji bhai*.

I would be a disgrace to Allah
If I choose race, creed or colour
Babu Kancha had to make a journey
For I too have sympathy
So it is a great privilege
To have such unique heritage
Fifty percent Africa fifty percent India, India.

I have [?] two holiday
Emancipation and arrival day
Since Fath Al Razack make that journey
One hundred and fifty years gone already.
(Babu Kancha)
Whether you're Hindu, Muslim or Christian
Let's walk this land hand in hand
We could only prosper if we try
*Jihaji bhai*, brotherhood of the boat
*Jihaji bhai*, brotherhood of the boat
*Jihaji bhai*.

For those who playing ignorant
Talking about true African descendant
If you want to know the truth
Take a trip back to your root
And somewhere on that journey
You go see a man in a *dhoti* [waist-wrapped cloth]
Saying he prayers in front of a *chandi, chandi*.

Then and only then you'll understand
What it is to be a cosmopolitan nation
There's no room for prejudice at all
United we stand, divided we fall
So [?] Trinbago
[?]
Let us live as one under the sky
*Jihaji bhai…*

Brother Marvin is both a calypsonian and a chutney singer who participates in calypso and chutney competitions. His text, "*Jihaji Bhai*", emphasizes a common experience: the voyage undertaken on the boats by the enslaved and indentured ancestors of the majority of the Trinidadian audience. His aim is to promote a sense of unity and he draws on a musical vocabulary (soca beat, *dholak* and *sitar* timbres, verse–chorus structure with refrains such as "Babu Kancha" sung by a female chorus) that is readily identified with disparate sections of the nation's population. All the elements of this musical vocabulary nevertheless fit together concordantly (within a tonic, subdominant, dominant harmonic structure).

*Jihajis* (shipmate or ship family) were linked by their experience of crossing the *kala pani* (the black water). The term *jihaji bhai* (ship brother) came to signify the bond of friendship forged between people who travelled on the same vessel from India to the Caribbean. The *jihaji* relation continued on arrival since many of the labourers travelling on the same ship were sent to the same plantation. This bond became a unifying force amongst Indians who came from diverse backgrounds. Bharath talks about meeting ships in the harbour in a gesture of solidarity (again in Mahabir's compilation of the personal accounts of first generation Indian labourers):

> anybody coming
> any ship coming
> me
> all of dem
> i go an meet e
> an cry
> bhaiya [brother] wha country you come from
> > (in Mahabir 1985, 100)

Sundar Popo's arrival day chutney song ("the Fatel Rozack came from India", see chapter 3) draws on the same kind of musical vocabulary used by Brother Marvin but it refers to the first ship that brought indentured labourers to Trinidad, and thereby draws attention to the specificity of the Indian-Caribbean journey.

The political intent informing ideas about unity is apparent in these song texts. In this respect, the singers Brother Marvin and Sundar Popo can be regarded, as Catherine Hall writes, as "telling stories of new identities . . . , enabling Caribbean peoples to recognize themselves as Africans and diasporized, as Indians and diasporized, imaginatively connected in complex ways to the histories of slavery and indenture" (Hall 1996, 69). Yet despite the political importance of these portrayals of unity, both the song texts and Hall's notion of uniform diasporas reveal homogenizing tendencies symptomatic of colonial discourses which have inspired a call for the development of multivocality in counternarratives, such as the voices of the native passengers on board the *Sheila* and of other members of the crew, if only they could be reclaimed, as well as that of Captain Angel. (Examples of critiques of the homogenizing enterprise include Bhaba 1996 [1983]; Frankenburg and Mani 1996 [1993].) Such multivocality is at any rate evident in the reception of *"Jihaji bhai"*. In Trinidad, discussions about the song revolved around artistic merit and whether or not it should have won the calypso competition (it came second). In the exchange which took place in the pages of the London based circular, *Soca News*, attention focused on the proper categorization of the song (chutney or calypso). Geraldine Bicette described *"Jihaji Bhai"* as a "special" chutney song:

When the song starts the only instruments to be heard are an Indian drum and a sitar. These are soon joined by Marvin's Caribbean vocals singing Swahili phrases of love and unity over the top. It is not until a few seconds later, when the rhythmic melody is finally put into place, that the audience is made aware of the song's dominant Caribbean influence. This complex combination of sounds is what makes the piece so aesthetically wonderful. The constant inter-twining of the three languages of Hindi, Swahili and English [is] both appro-priate and interesting. Thus, what we have here is not a song which simply deliv-ers a message, but a song which to a point stands as a message itself. (Bicette 1996, 4)

Bicette's contribution to *Soca News* prompted a response from a chutney promoter in London, Suresh Rambaran:

I read in your April issue an article by Geraldine Bicette and her interpretation of chutney music using Brother Marvin's song Jihaji Bhai (Brotherhood of the Boat) . . . This is indeed a lovely song with lyrics conveying a message of nation-al unity . . . However, it is not a chutney or even a soca chutney – it is a calyp-so. (Suresh [Rambaran] 1996, 6)

Chutney can be perceived as having its origins in folk traditions from particular regions (in north India), but it emerges as one of the sites in which contestations over local or national culture are played out (Reddock 1995), not only in Trinidad but also in Caribbean diasporic commentary.

## THE POLITICS OF LOCATION

Chutney emerges as a popular genre that is made up of diverse musical traditions and is a cultural expression of "interactive diversity". The aspect of diversity lies in the representation of chutney as an Indian-Caribbean form which serves to assert a particular ethnicity, identity, history and cultural space. It is interactive in being part of a Trinidadian, and on a broader level, Caribbean complex. Thus musicians are experimenting with new forms of chutney: chutney soca and ragga chutney (Terry Gajraj's collaboration with Apache Waria). The term "chutney" is one that is itself related to other Caribbean musics which are described as "hot". Like that other term which denotes a spicy condiment and a musical genre, "salsa", the term "chutney" has been used as a marketing and representational tool. This is why explanations regarding the origin of the term chutney are so different.

Ramsawak told me, "chutney is a fast beat song normally sung by women in days gone by and in those days it used to be called *lahara*". Ali explained, "because the music is hot too people started calling it chutney". Just as salsa drew on diverse Cuban forms, chutney is not a single genre of music. It is a composite of different traditions. There was no salsa before Fania Records promoted Cuban music in New York under that label. Chutney was used initially to describe Indian-Caribbean traditions, which were beginning to be recorded and performed in the 1970s. Chutney has not yet entered the mainstream of the global music marketplace but it is global in terms of being forged from diasporic traditions. Today those diasporas consist of the Indian-Caribbean as well as the Indian. As part of Caribbean popular culture, chutney is a cultural space which is primarily (although not exclusively) associated not with Indians in the Caribbean but with Indian-Caribbean nationals who draw on multiple and generalized images of India to situate themselves within specific historical frameworks in a Caribbean homeland.

The histories of chutney which locate musical practices as stemming from particular places outside of the Caribbean context have been central in making this association. Musical traditions are then "preserved" and performed by women in ritual ceremonies or held in the oral memory. These are seen as interacting with other musical traditions which likewise have their origins elsewhere. The musical dialogues in contemporary chutney, explored here in terms of particular combinations of instrumental timbres and club mixes, emerge in a Caribbean context. But these too are shaped by trends in various other arenas (for example, the Caribbean as a region, the World Music market, popular trends, and the music scenes in London, New York and Toronto).

Music in Trinidad is deeply implicated with political processes. As performances of multilocal belonging, chutney song texts often make explicit references to the dilemmas of cultural displacement as well as to the possibilities for cultural placement. Thinking here about the musical dialogues in chutney within the analytic framework(s) of postcolonial theory is not a privileging of the "postcolonial" but the highlighting of how the interactions and relationships between musical traditions in Trinidad serve as a vehicle for a political aspiration to national unity. Such a framework is apt, for chutney emerged on public stages in the post-colonial era as a specifically, although not exclusively, Indian-Caribbean popular music which contributed to the wider Caribbean musical scene. Analysis of stylistic features, of song texts, of instrumental timbre, and consideration of the different kinds of histories claimed for chutney demonstrate that simple models of cultural contact which focus on one-way processes of musical transmission or on ideas of preservation must be replaced by those which account for complex scenarios of exchange and incorporation. Musical dialogues in chutney reveal how music can operate as a medium for the reconceptualization of what constitutes contemporary Trinidadian society, the contestation of identities within the postcolonial state and interactions which do not result from simply conceived ideas of division (colonizer/colonized or between different ethnic groupings). Captain Angel's discourse told us about one kind of musical space in which Indian musical traditions were not simply trans-ported and transplanted. The sound world of the clipper ship *Sheila*, as it travelled from Calcutta to Trinidad, was a juxtaposition of musical traditions which must have shaped the musical conceptualizations of all who heard them. In its postcolonial context, contemporary musical dialogues in chutney likewise offer a commentary on the complexities of the politics of location.

# Notes

## INTRODUCTION

1. Until recently the *Fath Al Razak* (meaning the Victory of Allah the Provider) was known as the *Fatel Rozack*. Debate about the name of the ship began as soon as it had left Calcutta with the first shipment of Indian labourers to Trinidad. The London owners of estates in Trinidad wrote about the *Futlah Razan*. Other variants included *Fatel Rozack* and *Futtle Rozack*, see Samaroo 1995 for further discussion.

2. The Arya Samaj reformist movement was founded by Swami Dayananda Saraswati (1824–83) in the Punjab in 1875. Solidarity and equality amongst Hindus are stressed. It is a movement which has had a considerable influence on Indian diasporic populations, see Vertovec 1992.

3. This literature often attests to views such as those expressed by Miller. He notes that it is through ideas about ethnicity that "dualism as an explicit discourse is most clearly acknowledged in Trinidadian life" (1994, 286). This is a theme I shall return to in chapter 3.

4. I am grateful to John Cowley for sight of this discography.

5. The details for the particular collection referred to here are as follows: *Caribbean Voyage: The 1962 Field Recordings. East Indian Music in the West Indies*, Rounder 11661-1723-2.

# CHAPTER ONE

1. Rawatie Ali, transcribed from a taped interview, 12 July 1996, Trinidad.
2. James Ramsawak, transcribed from a taped interview, 30 July 1996, Trinidad.
3. Satnarine Balkaransingh, transcribed from a taped interview, 13 July 1996, Trinidad.
4. Sanatanist is a follower of Sanatan Dharm (literally, eternal duty) which represents a generalized form of Hinduism. This form of Hinduism evolved in India and overseas during the nineteenth century and is observed by the majority of the Indian diasporic populations. For more details about Sanatan Dharm with specific reference to Trinidad, see Vertovec 1992.
5. Terry Gajraj, transcribed from a taped interview, 29 May 1996, London.
6. Cecil Fonrose, transcribed from a taped interview, 22 July 1996, Trinidad.
7. Sundar Popo, transcribed from a taped interview, 22 July 1996, Trinidad.

# CHAPTER TWO

1. Sundar Popo, transcribed from a taped interview, 22 July 1996, Trinidad.
2. Satnarine Balkaransingh, information given at a taped interview, 13 July 1996, Trinidad.
3. Terry Gajraj, transcribed from a taped interview, 29 May 1996, London.
4. James Ramsawak, transcribed from a taped interview, 30 July 1996, Trinidad.
5. Cecil Fonrose, transcribed from a taped interview, 22 July 1996, Trinidad.
6. Robin Ramsaran, transcribed from a taped interview, June 1997, London.
7. Praimsingh, information given at a personal interview, 6 July 1996, Trinidad.

# CHAPTER THREE

1. The spelling "chutney" rather than "chatni" is itself an identification of the genre as Indian-Caribbean, not Indian.

2. An important socioeconomic change has been migration to urban centres and Manuel suggests this trend as being one reason for rapid change in the reception of tradition. He writes that "the flowering of the chutney scene has paralleled the increased movement of East Indians away from rural sugar plantations and into the urban mainstream" (Manuel 1995, 218). This certainly would have contributed to gaining performance spaces beyond rural Indian-Trinidadian enclaves but other important factors include shifting gender relations and increasingly visible political activity.

3. JMC is Jamaican Music Connection (alternatively known as Jamaica Me Crazy), a record label based in New York.

4. BLS Records is a recording company based in the Virgin Islands.

5. A record producer decided to issue a compact disc chutney compilation as part of the company's World Music label series (Steve Bunyan, Music Collection International, personal communication and interview, February 1998). This action was in response to a feature in the music press (Ramnarine 1997). To the record producer, chutney seemed to be one of those relatively unknown musics waiting to enter the World Music market. The tracks selected for the compact disc were ones that focused on depicting chutney in relation to wider performance spaces.

# CHAPTER FOUR

1. Rawatie Ali, transcribed from a taped interview, 12 July 1996, Trinidad.

2. There are several variants in Trinidad of the term *mathkorwa*. I follow Ramnath's *mathkor* in this chapter. Other variants include *mathkor*, *maticore* and *muti kurwa*.

3. Baloon, transcribed from a taped interview, 22 July 1996, Trinidad.

4. Satnarine Balkaransingh, transcribed from a taped interview, 13 July 1996, Trinidad.

5. A description of the barracks is found in the comments made by the

English mayor of San Fernando at a meeting in 1886. He described families living in a single room with few facilities and little privacy (see Williams 1964, 105–6).

6.  Terry Gajraj, transcribed from a taped interview, 29 May 1996, London.

7.  Sundar Popo, transcribed from a taped interview, 22 July 1996, Trinidad.

8.  Terry Gajraj's use of mathkor rhythms can be heard on track 2, "maticore mix", in the recording, *The Tun Tun Dance* with Terry Gajraj and Apache Waria, produced by JTS Records, no date given.

9.  Chutney dancing is seen as predominantly a female activity and professional dancers are women. Yet, men also dance at chutney shows just as they are now involved in singing chutney.

10. Zeno Obi Constance, information given at a personal interview, 15 July 1996, Trinidad.

11. Indra Ribeiro, information given at a personal interview, 17 July 1996, Trinidad.

## CHAPTER FIVE

1.  Captain Angel wrote the account many years after the voyage as a description of the "good old days of Clipper sailing ships". His intent was not to document the Indian experience but he does do so indirectly. While it provides one of the few eyewitness accounts of the transportation of Indians as labourers to the Caribbean, the document itself was reclaimed as part of Indian-Caribbean history almost by chance, see Ramchand and Samaroo 1995: afterword, for details.

2.  From Walcott's 1992 Nobel lecture. This is cited by Mintz who makes a point relevant to this discussion on musical dialogues in a postcolonial music that "the tragedy and the glory of Caribbean history" can be read in these words. "Writ small it is the tragedy and glory of the encounter of the entire non-Western world with the West. But in the Caribbean case, it happened long before it did anywhere else, and under conditions that would prevent its awful novelty from being recognised for what it was: a modernity that predated the modern" (Mintz 1996, 305).

3.  I am grateful to Martin Clayton for drawing Ghulam Raza Khan to

my attention.

4. This is a reference to Chalkdust's calypso of 1970, "Massa Day Done", which dealt with an incident at a Port of Spain social club to which a black American couple were denied access on the basis of their colour: "we used to boast about our land, saying that we have integration, we told the world that our country is an example of love and racial harmony. All that's now a fake, the country club issue made us wide awake, but that's a drop of water my friend in our ocean of discrimination . . ."

# Glossary

| | |
|---|---|
| abeer | the throwing of coloured water during the phagwa festival |
| agaa | paternal grandfather |
| agee | paternal grandmother |
| Arya Samaj | a reformist Hindu movement |
| baboo | honorific term (also became an expression of ridicule denoting Calcutta's *nouveaux riches*) |
| barahi | celebrations on the twelfth night after the birth of a child |
| bembe | santeria party in Cuba, the term also refers to the drums played |
| bhajan | popular Hindu religious song |
| bhandra | British–South Asian popular music based on Punjab folk harvest festival genres |
| bhowji | sister-in-law |
| biraha | North Indian folk music genre also performed in Trinidad |
| canboulay | from the French *cannes brûlées* (burnt caners); carnival music and dance |
| caphra | cotton suit |
| chacha | uncle |
| chatak | spice |
| chatti | celebration which takes place six days after the birth of a child |

| | |
|---|---|
| chowpaies | songs or poems of four lines |
| chowtal | songs sang in praise of Krishna |
| chulha | stove |
| dhantal | percussion instrument consisting of an iron or steel rod struck by a horseshoe-shaped beater |
| dholak | small barrel drum |
| divali | Hindu festival of lights |
| harmonium | a hand-pumped keyboard instrument |
| Hosay | Muslim festival originating from the circumstances which led to the martyrdom of grandsons of the prophet Mohammed |
| Jatra | Indian folk theatrical form |
| kala pani | black water |
| lahara | Hindi: spice |
| lawa | parching of rice to use in a Hindu wedding ceremony |
| mandir | Hindu temple |
| mathkor | religious celebration which is part of Sanatanist Hindu weddings |
| naggara | small kettledrum |
| nana | maternal grandfather |
| nanee | maternal grandmother |
| parang | song sung in Spanish in Trinidad during Christmas |
| phagwa | spring festival of colours |
| phoulourie | a fried snack made with flour, split peas and other seasonings |
| picong | from the French word *piquant* – to hurl jokes or insults; often used in calypso song texts |
| pundit | Hindu priest |
| raag | term that refers to a system that encompasses melodic/pitch elements in Indian music |
| ragga | short for raggamuffin: a style of Jamaican dancehall music that developed during the 1980s |
| ramlila | performance of episodes from the Ramayana |
| salsa | a popular music and dance derived from Cuban *son*, and developed in New York |
| santeria | Yoruba-derived African-Cuban religion |
| ska | Jamaican popular music from the 1960s characterized by offbeat emphasis |

| | |
|---|---|
| soca | popular dance music in Trinidad |
| sohar | song sang to celebrate the birth of a child |
| son | popular Cuban music and dance genre |
| taal | term that refers to metric structure (rhythmic cycle) in Indian music |
| tabla | asymmetrical pair of tuned, hand played drums |
| tassa | kettledrum |
| zouk | popular dance music in Martinique, St Lucia, Dominica and Guadeloupe |

# References

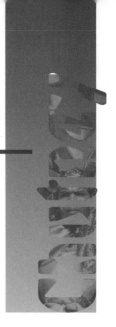

Ahyoung, Selwyn E. 1977. "The Music of Trinidad". BA thesis. University of Indiana.

Alexander, G. 1996. "Chutney Adds Its Spice to Our Cultural Evolution". *Trinidad Guardian,* 11 February 1996, 2.

Ali, S. 1995. "Indian Women and the Retention of Social Institutions in Trinidad 1870–1940s". Paper presented at the conference Challenge and Change: The Indian Diaspora in Its Historical and Contemporary Contexts, University of the West Indies, Trinidad.

Alleyne, Mervyn. 1988. *Roots of Jamaican Culture.* London: Pluto Press.

Banerjee, Sumanta. 1989. *The Parlour and the Streets: Elite and Popular Culture in Nineteenth Century Calcutta.* Calcutta: Seagull Books.

Baksh-Soodeen, R. 1991. "Power, Gender and Chutney". *Trinidad and Tobago Review* (February): 7.

Baptiste, Rhona. 1993. *Trinitalk: A Dictionary of Words and Proverbs of Trinidad and Tobago.* Port of Spain: Caribbean Information Systems and Services.

Baumann, G. 1990. "The Re-invention of Bhangra: Social Change and Aesthetic Shifts in Punjabi Music in Britain". *World of Music* 32, no. 2: 81–98.

Bennett, Herman L. 1989. "The Challenge to the Postcolonial State: A Case Study of the February Revolution in Trinidad". In *The Modern Caribbean*, ed. F. W. Knight and C. A. Palmer, 129–46. Chapel Hill and London: University of North Carolina Press.

Bhabha, Homi. 1996 [1983]. "The Other Question". In *Contemporary Postcolonial Theory: A Reader*, ed. P. Mongia, 37–54. London: Arnold.

Bicette, Geraldine. 1996. "Soca Rite Back". *Soca News* 3: 4.

Bissoondialsingh, T. 1973. *Dhrupad Singing in Trinidad.* Trinidad: Bharatiya Vidya Sansthaan.

Brah, Avtar. 1996. *Cartographies of Diaspora: Contesting Identities*. London: Routledge.

Brandily, Monique. 1984. "Dandtal". In *The New Grove Dictionary of Musical Instruments*, vol. 1, ed. Stanley Sadie, 541. London: Macmillan.

Brereton, Bridget. 1993. "Social Organisation and Class, Racial and Cultural Conflict in Nineteenth Century Trinidad". In *Trinidad Ethnicity*, ed. Kevin Yelvington, 33–55. London and Basingstoke: Macmillan.

Capwell, Charles. 1993. "The Interpretation of History and the Foundations of Authority in the Visnupur Gharana of Bengal". In *Ethnomusicology and Modern Music History*, ed. Stephen Blum, Philip V. Bohlman, and Daniel M. Neuman, 95-102. Urbana and Chicago: University of Illinois Press.

Césaire, Aimé. 1993 [1950]. "Discourse on Colonialism". In *Colonial Discourse and Postcolonial Theory: A Reader*, ed. P. Williams and L. Chrisman, 172–80. New York: Harvester Wheatsheaf.

Chadee, A. M. 1995. "The Chutney Phenomenon". *Sunday Express*, 28 May 1995, 20–21.

Chakrabarty, Dipesh. 1996 [1992]. "Postcoloniality and the Artifice of History: Who Speaks for 'Indian' Pasts?" In *Contemporary Postcolonial Theory: A Reader*, ed. P. Mongia, 223–47. London: Arnold.

Clarke, Colin. 1993. "Spatial Pattern and Social Interaction among Creoles and Indians in Trinidad and Tobago". In *Trinidad Ethnicity*, ed. Kevin Yelvington, 116–35. London and Basingstoke: Macmillan.

Clifford, James. 1988. *The Predicament of Culture: Twentieth-Century Ethnography, Literature, and Art*. Cambridge, Mass.: Harvard University Press.

Constance, Zeno Obi. 1991. *Tassa, Chutney and Soca: The East Indian Contribution to Calypso*. Trinidad: San Fernando.

Cowley, John. 1996. *Carnival, Canboulay and Calypso: Traditions in the Making*. Cambridge: Cambridge University Press.

Cudjoe, Selwyn R. 1985. Foreword. In *The Still Cry: Personal Accounts of East Indians in Trinidad and Tobago during Indentureship 1845–1917*, ed. Noor K. Mahabir, 9–33. Tacarigua: Calaloux Publications.

Dabydeen, David, and Brinsley Samaroo, eds. 1987. *India in the Caribbean*. London: Hansib.

Dabydeen, David, and Brinsley Samaroo, eds. 1996. *Across the Dark Waters: Ethnicity and Indian Identity in the Caribbean*. London and Basingstoke: Macmillan Education.

Deosaran, Ramesh. 1987. "The 'Caribbean Man': A Study of the Psychology of Perception and the Media". In *India in the Caribbean*, ed. David Dabydeen and Brinsley Samaroo, 81–117. London: Hansib.

Deosaran, Ramesh. 1995. "Voices of the Past, Visions of the Future". In *In Celebration of 150 Years of the Indian Contribution to Trinidad and*

*Tobago,* vol. 2, ed. Brinsley Samaroo et al., 175–82. Port of Spain: Historical Publications.

Desroches, Monique. 1996. *Tambours des Dieux: Musique et Sacrifice d'Origine Tamoule en Martinique.* Montreal: Harmattan.

Dick, Alastair. 1984. "Dholak" and "Kartal". In The New Grove Dictionary of Musical Instruments, vols. 1 and 2, ed. Stanley Sadie, 1: 562 and 2: 361–62. London: Macmillan.

Dudley, S. 1996. "Judging 'By the Beat': Calypso versus Soca". *Ethnomusicology* 40, no. 2: 269–98.

Frankenburg, Ruth, and Lata Mani. 1996 [1993]. "Crosscurrents, Crosstalk: Race, 'Postcoloniality' and the Politics of Location". In Contemporary Postcolonial Theory: A Reader, ed. P. Mongia, 347–64. London: Arnold.

Goodman, Jane. 1998. "Singers, Saints, and the Construction of Postcolonial Subjectivities in Algeria". *Ethos* 26, no. 2: 204–28.

Grierson, George A. 1884. "Some Bihari Folk-songs". *Journal of the Royal Asiatic Society of Great Britain and Ireland* 16: 196–246.

Grierson, George A. 1885. *Bihar Peasant Life, being a Discursive Catalogue of the Surroundings of the People of that Province.* London: Trubner and Co.

Grierson, George A. 1886. "Some Bhojpuri Folk-songs". *Journal of the Royal Asiatic Society of Great Britain and Ireland* 18: 201–67.

Guilbault, Jocelyn, et al. 1993. *Zouk: World Music in the West Indies.* Chicago: Chicago University Press.

Hall, Catherine. 1996. "Histories, Empires and the Post-colonial Moment". In *The Postcolonial Question: Common Skies, Divided Horizons,* ed. I. Chambers and L. Curti, 65–77. London and New York: Routledge.

Hall, Stuart. 1996. "Cultural Identity and Diaspora". In *Contemporary Postcolonial Theory: A Reader,* ed. Padmini Mongia, 110–21. London: Arnold.

Haraksingh, Kusha. 1987. "Control and Resistance among Indian Workers: A Study of Labour on the Sugar Plantations of Trinidad 1875–1917". In *India in the Caribbean,* ed. David Dabydeen and Brinsley Samaroo, 61–79. London: Hansib.

Hebdige, Dick. 1987. *Cut 'n' Mix: Culture, Identity and Caribbean Music.* London and New York: Routledge.

Henry, Edward O. 1973. "The Meanings of Music in a North Indian Village". PhD diss., Michigan State University.

Henry, Edward O. 1976. "The Variety of Music in a North Indian Village: Reassessing Cantometrics". *Ethnomusicology* 20, no. 1: 49–66.

Herskovits, M. J., and F. S. Herskovits. 1947. *Trinidad Village.* New York: Octagon Books.

Hill, Donald R. 1993. *Calypso Calaloo: Early Carnival Music in Trinidad.* Gainesville: University Press of Florida.

Jaggi, Maya. 1995. "Their Long Voyage Home". *Trinidad Guardian*, 16 December, 29.

Jairazbhoy, Nazir. 1993. "India". In *The New Grove Handbooks in Music: Ethnomusicology: Historical and Regional Studies*, ed. Helen Myers, 274–93. London: Macmillan.

Kanhai, Rosanne. 1995. "The Masala Stone Sings: Indo-Caribbean Women Coming into Voice". Paper presented at the conference, Challenge and Change: The Indian Diaspora in Its Historical and Contemporary Contexts, University of the West Indies, Trinidad.

Kapchan, Deborah A. 1994. "Moroccan Female Performers Defining the Social Body". *Journal of American Folklore* 107, no. 423: 82–105.

Kartomi, Margaret J. 1981. "The Processes and Results of Musical Culture Contact: A Discussion of Terminology and Concepts". *Ethnomusicology* 25, no. 2: 227–49.

Klass, Morton. 1961. *East Indians in Trinidad: A Study of Cultural Persistence.* Prospect Heights, Ill.: Waveland Press.

Koskoff, Ellen. 1993. "Miriam Sings Her Song: The Self and the Other in Anthropological Discourse". In *Musicology and Difference: Gender and Sexuality in Music Scholarship*, ed. Ruth Solie, 149–63. Berkeley, Los Angeles and London: University of California Press.

Koskoff, Ellen, ed. 1989. *Women and Music in Cross-Cultural Perspective.* Chicago: University of Illinois Press.

Kurup, Rama D. 1995. "Life on a Sugar Estate". In *In Celebration of 150 Years of the Indian Contribution to Trinidad and Tobago,* Vol. 2, ed. Brinsley Samaroo et al., 38–40. Port of Spain: Historical Publications.

Levine, Lawrence W. 1977. *Black Culture and Black Consciousness: Afro-American Folk Thought from Slavery to Freedom.* Oxford: Oxford University Press.

Lowenthal, David. 1972. *West Indian Societies.* Oxford: Oxford University Press.

Mahabir, Noor K. 1985. *The Still Cry: Personal Accounts of East Indians in Trinidad and Tobago during the Period of Indentureship, 1845–1917.* Tacarigua: Calaloux Publications.

Maharaj, Shivannand. 1994. "The Development of Indian Classical Music in Trinidad and Tobago in the Twentieth Century". BA thesis. University of West Indies.

Malm, Krister, and Roger Wallis. 1992. *Media Policy and Music Activity.* London: Routledge.

Mangru, Basdeo. 1987. "The Sex Ratio Disparity and its Consequences under the Indenture in British Guiana". In *India in the Caribbean*, ed. David Dabydeen and Brinsley Samaroo, 211–30. London: Hansib.

Manuel, Peter. 1988. *Popular Musics of the Non-Western World: An Introductory Survey.* Oxford: Oxford University Press.

Manuel, Peter. 1993. *Cassette Culture: Popular Music and Technology in North India*. Chicago and London: University of Chicago Press.

Manuel, Peter. 1995. *Caribbean Currents: Caribbean Music from Rumba to Reggae*. Philadelphia: Temple University Press.

Manuel, Peter. 1997–98. "Music, Identity, and Images of India in the Indo-Caribbean Diaspora". *Asian Music* 29, no. 1: 17–35.

Marcus, Scott. 1992. "Recycling Indian Film-songs: Popular Music as a Source of Melodies for North Indian Folk Musicians". *Asian Music* 24, no. 1: 101–10.

McDaniel, Lorna. 1998. *The Big Drum Ritual of Carriacou: Praisesongs in Rememory of Flight*. Gainesville: University Press of Florida.

Miller, Daniel. 1994. *Modernity, an Ethnographic Approach: Dualism and Mass Consumption in Trinidad*. Oxford: Berg.

Mintz, Sydney. 1985. *Sweetness and Power: The Place of Sugar in Modern History*. London: Viking.

Mintz, Sydney. 1996. "Enduring Substances, Trying Theories: The Caribbean Region as Oikoumene". *Journal of the Royal Anthropological Institute* 2: 289–311.

Mishra, Vijay, and Bob Hodge. 1993 [1991]. "What Is Post(-)colonialism?" In *Colonial Discourse and Postcolonial Theory: A Reader*, ed. P. Williams and L. Chrisman, 276–90. New York: Harvester Wheatsheaf.

Moodie-Kublalsingh, Sylvia. 1994. *The Cocoa Panyols of Trinidad: An Oral Record*. London: British Academic Press.

Myers, Helen. 1980. "Trinidad and Tobago". In *The Groves Dictionary of Music and Musicians*, ed. Stanley Sadie, 146–50. London: Macmillan.

Myers, Helen. 1984. "*Felicity, Trinidad: The Musical Portrait of a Hindu Village*". PhD diss., University of Edinburgh.

Myers, Helen. 1993a. "Indian, East Indian and West Indian Music in Felicity, Trinidad". In *Ethnomusicology and Modern Music History*, ed. Stephen Blum, Philip V. Bohlman and Daniel M. Neuman, 231–41. Urbana and Chicago: University of Illinois Press.

Myers, Helen. 1993b. "The West Indies". In *The New Grove Handbooks in Music: Ethnomusicology: Historical and Regional Studies,* ed. Helen Myers, 461–71. London: Macmillan.

Myers, Helen. 1998. *Music of Hindu Trinidad: Songs from the India Diaspora*. Chicago and London: Chicago University Press.

Neuman, Daniel. 1990. *The Life of Music in North India: The Organization of an Artistic Tradition*. Chicago: Chicago University Press.

Olwig, Karen Fog, and Kirsten Hastrup, eds. 1997. *Siting Culture: The Shifting Anthropological Object*. London: Routledge.

Ospina, Hernando Calvo. 1995. *Salsa: Havana Heat, Bronx Beat*, trans. Nick Caistor. London: Latin American Bureau.

Owen, Barbara, and Alistair Dick. 1984. "Harmonium". In *The New Grove Dictionary of Musical Instruments*, vol. 2, ed. Stanley Sadie, 131. London: Macmillan.

Patasar, Mungal. 1995. "Modern Trends in Indo-Trinidad Music". In *In Celebration of 150 Years of the Indian Contribution to Trinidad and Tobago*, vol. 2, ed. Brinsley Samaroo et al., 75–85. Port of Spain: Historical Publications.

Persad, R. 1988. *Rites, Rituals and Customs Associated with the Hindu Marriage Ceremony in Trinidad and Tobago*. Curepe, Trinidad: Praimsingh's Puja Shop.

Phillips, Daphne. 1998. "Carnival and Chutney in Contemporary TT". *Newsday* 15 April, 10–11.

Post, Jennifer C. 1994. "Erasing the Boundaries between Public and Private in Women's Performance Traditions". In *Cecilia Reclaimed: Feminist Perspectives on Gender and Music*, ed. S. C. Cook and J. S. Tsou, 35–51. Urbana and Chicago: University of Illinois Press.

Powers, Harold. 1980. "India". In *The Grove Dictionary of Music and Musicians*, ed. Stanley Sadie, 69–141. London: Macmillan.

Poynting, Jeremy. 1987. "East Indian Women in the Caribbean: Experience and Voice". In *India in the Caribbean*, ed. David Dabydeen and Brinsley Samaroo, 231–63. London: Hansib.

Ramaya, Narsaloo. 1990. "Chutney Singing: Its Origin and Development in Trinidad and Tobago". Manuscript, West Indies Collection, University of West Indies Library, Trinidad.

Rambaran, Suresh. 1996. "Soca Rite Back". *Soca News* 5: 6–7.

Ramchand, Ken, and Brinsley Samaroo, eds. 1995. *A Return to the Middle Passage: The Clipper Ship Sheila*. Port of Spain: Caribbean Information Systems and Services.

Ramnarine, Tina K. 1997. "Chutney Time". *Folk Roots* 19, nos. 2 and 3: 43–45.

Ramnath, Harry. n.d. *India Came West*. Marabella: Ramnath.

Ramoutar, Paras. 1996. "From Karhai to Sonny Mann". *Sunday Express* (supplement), 26 May, 8.

Ravi-Ji. 1996. "Neglecting Real Musical Wealth". *Trinidad Guardian*, 11 February, 13.

Reddock, Rhoda. 1995. "Contestations Over National Culture in Trinidad and Tobago: Considerations of Ethnicity, Class and Gender". In *Contemporary Issues in Social Science: A Caribbean Perspective*, ed. Ramesh Deosaran and Nasser Mustapha, 106–45. St Augustine, Trinidad: Ansa McAl Psychological Research Centre, University of the West Indies.

Reyes-Schramm, Adelaida. 1990. "Music and the Refugee Experience". *World of Music* 32, no. 3: 3–21.

Ribeiro, Indra. 1992. "The Phenomenon of Chutney Singing in Trinidad and

Tobago: The Functional Value of a Social Phenomenon". BA thesis. University of the West Indies, St Augustine.

Samaroo, Brinsley. 1987. "Two Abolitions: African Slavery and East Indian Indentureship". In *India in the Caribbean*, ed. David Dabydeen and Brinsley Samaroo, 25–41. London: Hansib.

Samaroo, Brinsley. 1995. "The First Ship: The Fath Al Razak". In *In Celebration of 150 Years of the Indian Contribution to Trinidad and Tobago*, vol. 2, ed. Brinsley Samaroo et al., 1–14. Port of Spain: Historical Publications.

Samaroo, Brinsley. 1996. "The Indian Origins of Caribbean Indian Music". Paper presented at the 1996 seminar of the Sangeet Society.

Samlal, M. 1972. *Indian Folk Songs in Trinidad*. Trinidad: Bharatiya Vidya Sansthaan.

Seecharan, Clem. 1997. '*Tiger in the Stars*': *The Anatomy of Indian Achievement in British Guiana 1919–1929*. London and Basingstoke: Macmillan Education.

Selvon, Sam. 1987. "Three into One Can't Go: East Indian, Trinidadian, Westindian". In *India in the Caribbean*, ed. David Dabydeen and Brinsley Samaroo, 13–24. London: Hansib.

Simmonds, Austin W. 1959. *Pan and Panmen*. Port of Spain, Trinidad: Department of Extra-Mural Studies, University of the West Indies.

Slawek, Stephen M. 1993. "Ravi Shankar as Mediator between a Traditional Music and Modernity". In *Ethnomusicology and Modern Music History*, ed. Stephen Blum, Philip V. Bohlman and Daniel M. Neuman, 161–80. Urbana and Chicago: University of Illinois Press.

Slobin, Mark. 1993. *Subcultural Sounds: Micromusics of the West*. Hanover: Wesleyan University Press.

Small, Essiba. 1996. "The Art of Biraha". *Sunday Express*, 5 May, 4.

Small, Christopher. 1987. *Music of the Common Tongue*. London: Calder.

Spottswood, Dick, and John Cowley. 1996. "A Discography of East Indian Recordings from the English-speaking West Indies". Manuscript.

Stokes, Martin. 1992. *The Arabesk Debate: Music and Musicians in Modern Turkey*. Oxford: Clarendon Press.

Stokes, Martin. 1994. Introduction. In *Ethnicity, Identity and Music: The Musical Construction of Place*, ed. M. Stokes, 1–27. Oxford: Berg.

Stuempfle, Stephen. 1995. *The Steelband Movement: The Forging of a National Art in Trinidad and Tobago*. Philadelphia: University of Pennsylvania Press.

Treitler, Leo. 1989. *Music and the Historical Imagination*. Cambridge, Mass.: Harvard University Press.

Treitler, Leo. 1993. "Gender and Other Dualities of Music History". In *Musicology and Difference: Gender and Sexuality in Music Scholarship*, ed. Ruth Solie, 23–45. Berkeley, Los Angeles and London: University of California Press.

Turino, Thomas. 1993. *Moving Away from Silence: Music of the Peruvian Altiplano and the Experience of Urban Migration*. Chicago: Chicago University Press.

Van Koningsbruggen, Peter. 1997. *Trinidad Carnival: A Quest for National Identity*. London and Basingstoke: Macmillan Education.

Vertovec, Steven. 1992. *Hindu Trinidad: Religion, Ethnicity and Socio-Economic Change*. London and Basingstoke: Macmillan.

Wade, Bonnie. 1980. "India". In *The Grove Dictionary of Music and Musicians*, ed. Stanley Sadie, 147–58. London: Macmillan.

Walcott, Derek. 1992. *The Antilles*. New York: Farrar Straus Giroux.

Warner, Keith Q. 1993. "Ethnicity and the Contemporary Calypso". In *Trinidad Ethnicity*, ed. Kevin Yelvington, 275–91. London and Basingstoke: Macmillan.

Williams, Eric. 1964 [1962]. *History of the People of Trinidad and Tobago*. London: Andre Deutsch.

Wood, Donald. 1968. *Trinidad in Transition: The Years After Slavery*. Oxford: Oxford University Press.

Yelvington, Kevin A. 1993. "Introduction: Trinidad Ethnicity". In *Trinidad Ethnicity*, ed. K. Yelvington, 1–32. London and Basingstoke: Macmillan.

## Sound Recordings

Ali, Rawatie. *Mangal Vivah Geet*. Private recording sponsored by Miracle Foodworld Ltd. Debe [n.d.].

Dindial, Jairam. "We Voting UNC". In *Jairam Dindial, Classical and Chutney*. Cassette. Praimsingh Sangeet Bhavan. Trinidad 1995.

Gajraj, Terry. "Tun Tun Dance" and "Maticore Mix". In *The Tun Tun Dance*. Cassette. JTS Records, distributed by JMC Records Inc. [n.d.].

Gajraj, Terry. "Guyana Baboo". Cassette [no details]. 1994.

Garcia, Chris. "Chutney Bacchanal". In *Chris Garcia: Chutney Bacchanal*. Cassette. JMC Records Inc. JMC-1120. New York 1996.

Lomax, Alan. The 1962 Recordings. *Caribbean Voyage. East Indian Music in the West Indies*. CD. Rounder 11661-1723-2. 1999.

Mann, Sonny. "Loota La". In *Soca Carnival 96*. CD. Tattoo Records Ltd 960102. London 1996.

Mann, Sonny. "Loota La Remix". In *Caribbean Party Rhythm* 1. Rituals Label CR3397. 1996.

Popo, Sundar. "Phoulourie". In *Classic Sundar Popo and JMC Triveni*. Cassette. JMC Records Inc. JMCCT-1082. New York 1994.

Popo, Sundar. "Indian Arrival" and "Cold Water". In *Cool Yourself with Cold Water*. Cassette. JMC Records Inc. JMC-1113. New York 1995.

Rampartap, Heeralal. "Chutney Possy". In *Heeralal Rampartap*. Cassette. MC Records MC0013. Trinidad 1995.

Ramsaran, Amina. "Eh Bhaiya Bhowji". In *Bina Bolai: Amina Ramsaran*. Cassette. Praimsingh Sangeet Bhavan. Trinidad [n.d.].

Ramsawak, James. "Hindi Kawali". In *Master Ramsewack and B. Gopis East Indian Orchestra*. Decca DE-16505. Port of Spain 1940.

Ramsawak, James. "Dadha" In Master Ramsewack and B. Gopis East Indian Orchestra. Decca DE-16505. Port of Spain 1940.

Sparrow, Mighty. "Marajhin". In *Sparrow's Dance Party*. Cassette. BLS Records BLS-1015. US Virgin Islands 1992.

Yankaran, Anand. "If Your Mammy Like ah Sadine" and "Club Mix". In *Party Time*. Cassette. JMC Records Inc. JMC-1087. New York 1994.

Yankaran, Anand. "Guyana Kay Dulahin". In *Chutney in the House*. Cassette. JMC Records Inc. JMC-1112. New York 1996.

# Index

Abeer, 151
Adesh, H. S., 9, 133
Agaa, 151
Agee, 151
Al Razak, Fath, 8, 146
Ali, Rawatie, 21, 24, 147, 148
Angel, W. H., 2, 149
Arya Samaj, 9, 146, 151

Babla, 10
Baboo, 52, 151
Bahar, Mastana, 21
Balkaransingh, Mondira, 9
Baloon, 104, 148
*Barahi*, 18, 151
Belfon, Denise, 44
Bembe, 4, 151
"Bengalee Baboo", 51
*Bhajans*, 74, 151
Bhandra, 151
*Bhangra*, 97
Bhojpuri, 9, 43
*Bhowji*, 55, 151
Bihar, 9
Bihari, 58
*Biraha*, 47, 66, 151
Black Power movement, 139
BLS records, 88, 148

Bluebird Recording Company, 17
British Broadcasting Corporation, 133
Brother Marvin, 142
Brotherhood of the Boat, 136
*Byah ke git*, 106

Calcutta, 2
Calypso, 4, 16
Canboulay, 16, 151
Caphra, 151
Carnival/Cultural Judges Association
    of Trinidad and Tobago, 79
Carnival institute, 80
Caste system, 10
Césaire, Aimé, 119
Chacha, 151
Chadee, Ann Marie, 109
Chamar caste, 15
*Chatak*, 21, 151
*Chatni*, 16
*Chatti*, 18, 151
Chattopadhyay, Bankim Chandra, 54
Chowpaies, 152
*Chowtal*, 74, 152
Chulha, 152
Chutney, 1
    crossover developments, 92
    dance, 53

genealogy, 26
London, 6, 10, 92–97
New York, 10
origins, 12
performance venue, 1
reggae, 15
ritual, 26
soca, 15
song composition, 70
song texts, 51
texts, 55
Toronto, 10
variations, 15
"Chutney Bacchanal", 56
Chutney monarch, 54
"Chutney Possey", 40, 56
Clarinet, 54
Clipper ship, 2
Club mixes, 13
Cocoa panyols, 22
"Cold Water", 55
Composition, 48, 69
Continuity and change, 23
Cowbell, 31
Creolization, 5
Cultural persistence, 132
Cultural transformation, 5

*Danda*, 65
*Dandtal*, 63
Debain, Alexandre Francois, 48
Debe, 17, 23
Decca Recording Company, 17
Decolonization, 139
Devotional songs, 4, 9
*Dhantal*, 12, 15, 34, 63–68, 152
*Dholak*, 12, 15, 47, 63, 152
Diaspora, 1, 132
   Indian-Caribbean, 10, 11
Diatonicism, 49
Dictator, 114
Dindial, Jairam, 48, 74
Divali, 152
Dominica, 4
Drum machines, 63, 77

Drupatee, 40
Dub, 13
Dulaha, 83
Dulahin, 83, 92

Ebony, 114
"Eh Bhaiya Bhowji", 43–44
Electronic instruments, 63
Emperor Akbar, 133
Ethnicity, 6

Family structures, 117
Fazal, 64
Female sexuality, 113
Film music, 4
Films, 9
Folk music, 116
Fonrose, Cecil, 35, 66, 147
Fragmentation, 120

G and H Promotions, 93
Gajraj, Terry, 26, 50, 147, 149
Garcia, Chris, 56
General Grant, 44
*Gita*, 66
Glass, Philip, 134
Goirapa, 108
Grierson, George, 46, 101
Guadeloupe, 4
Guitars, 77
Guyana, 10
"Guyana Baboo", 27, 50
"Guyana Kay Dulahin", 61

Harmonic structure, 50
Harmonium, 12, 15, 54, 63, 152
Hijras, 105
Hindi, 60
Hindu Women's Association, 112, 117
Hosay, 152
Hybridity, 120

Identity, 6
Indentureship, 6
Indian Council for Cultural

Relations, 126
Indian culture, preservation of, 5
Indian folk traditions, 4
Indianness, 6, 9, 19, 132
Instrumentation, 35, 63–68
Interactive diversity, 137, 144
Intercultural networks, 96
Interethnic interactions, 107
Intergender interactions, 107

Jamaica Music Connection, 73, 148
*Jatra*, 53, 152

*Kaharava*, 66
*Kaherwa*, 61
*Kala pani*, 51, 152
Kanchan, 10
*Kartal*, 65
Keyboards, 77
Khan, Ghulam Raza, 131, 149
*Khemta*, 54
Killer, 114
Kinship relations, 55, 85

*Lachari*, 106
*Lahara*, 21, 152
*Lawa*, 18, 152
Local music, 29
Lomax, Alan, 17
London, 6, 10, 92–97
London Policy Unit, 93
"Loota La", 43, 56
Lord Kitchener, 133
Lord Shorty, 114
*Lota*, 64
Lucknow court, 130

Maha Bharat, 9
Maharaj, Shivannand, 126
Maharaj, Suresh, 74
Mandir, 152
*Ma[n]jeera*, 65
Mann, Sonny, 43, 44, 55
Maraj, Bhadase, 72
"Marajhin", 34

Marley, Bob, 140
Martinique, 4
*Mathkor*, 12, 18, 29, 152
Maticore, 29
Melodic cells, 48
Melodic composition, 46
Melodic movement, 48
Melodic range, 48
Melodic structure, 61
Melodies, 43
Melody, 114
Melody Makers, 96
Mento, 4
Merengue, 4
Metric structure, 61
Mighty Sparrow, 34, 87, 114
Migration, 76
Ministry of Community Development,
    Cultural, and Women's Affairs, 79
Mohammed, Moean, 21, 71
Multilocal belonging, 1
Music history, 11
Musical biographies, 96
Musical difference, 3
Musical exchange, 3
Musical exchanges, 99
Musical spaces, 133

*Naggara*, 66, 152
Nana, 152
Nanee, 152
"Nanee Nana", 39
National Association of Chutney
    Artists of Trinidad and Tobago, 79
National Chutney Monarch compe-
    tition, 79
*Nautch*, 66
*Nauthaki*, 66
New York, 10
North India, 63

Oral testimonies, 22
Oral transmission, 69
Original Pioneers, 96

Panday, Basdeo, 36, 98

Parang, 4, 152
Patasar, Mungal, 124
Pawar, Pratap, 9
Pawar, Priya, 9
People's National Movement, 139
Persad, Rajkumar Krishna, 9
Phagwa, 152
Phillips, Daphne, 79
Phoulourie, 152
"Phoulourie Bina Chutney", 40
Picong, 54, 152
Pitch range, 61
Popo, Sundar, 10, 37, 43, 84, 147, 149
Postcolonial subjectivities, 19
Praimsingh, 44, 73
Press reports, 76
*Puja* shops, 64
*Pundit*, 12, 152

*Raag*, 130, 152
Radio, 22
"Ram Bolo", 36
Ramaya, Narsaloo, 122
Ramayan, 66
Ramayana, 9
Rambaran, Suresh, 93
Ramcharan, Lilly, 40
Ramgoonai, Drupatee, 77–78, 84
Ramlila, 152
Ramnath, Harry, 101
Rampartap, Heeralal, 40
Ramsaran, Amina, 43, 55, 74
Ramsaran, Robin, 147
Ramsawak, James, 21, 39, 68, 147
Rap, 4, 13
Ras Shorty I, 113
Rastafarianism, 4
Ravi Shankar, 134
Recordings, 17
Reggae, 4, 13
Reggae chutney, 15
Religious songs, 67
Representation, 19
Rhythmic structure, 61

Ribeiro, Indra, 116, 149
Rikki Jai, 137
Rum-shop songs, 67
Rumba, 4

Sai Baba, 9
Salsa, 40, 152
Samaroo, 130
Sanatan Dharm, 101
Sanatanist Hindu, 25
Sankar, 114
Santeria, 152
*Sarangi*, 65
Satnarine, 9, 147, 148
Saxophone, 63
Sea shanties, 2, 3
Shankar, Ravi, 134
*Sheila*, 2, 133
*Shikhat*, 116–117
Shiv Nandan Laal Raay, 59
*Sitar*, 65
Ska, 4, 152
Soca, 93, 153
Soca chutney, 15
Sohar, 153
Sokah, 113
*Son*, 4, 136, 153
Sound recordings, 71
St Lucia, 4
Steelband, 15
Sugar plantations, 2
Surinam, 10
Swami Haridass, 133
Syllabic settings, 44

*Taal*, 61, 130, 153
*Tabla*, 47, 153
*Tanpura*, 54
Tansen, 133
*Tassa*, 12, 15, 153
Timbres, 40
Toronto, 10
Trinbago Unified Calypsonians Organization, 79
Trumpet, 63

Tun Tun, 27

Udey, Gopal, 54
Uttar Pradesh, 9

Victor Recording Company, 17
*Viraha*, 65, 66

Wajid Ali Shah, 130
Walcott, Derek, 120, 149

"We Voting UNC", 48
Wedding ceremony, 12
Williams, Eric, 139
*Windrush*, 132–133
Wining, 75
World Music, 79, 88

Yankaran, Anand, 61

Zouk, 4, 153